Hirst and Rhodes

HIRST AND RHODES

A. A. THOMSON

Introduction by J. M. Kilburn

THE PAVILION LIBRARY

First published in Great Britain 1959

Copyright © A. A. Thomson 1959
Introduction copyright © J. M. Kilburn 1986

First published in the Pavilion Library in 1986 by
Pavilion Books Limited
196 Shaftesbury Avenue, London WC2H 8JL
in association with Michael Joseph Limited
44 Bedford Square, London WC1B 3DP

British Library Cataloguing in Publication Data
Thomson, A. A.
Hirst and Rhodes.
1. Hirst, George Herbert   2. Rhodes, Wilfred
3. Cricket players—Biography
I. Title
796.35′8′0922   GV915.H/

ISBN 1 85145 024 6
ISBN 1 85145 025 4 paperback

Printed and bound in Great Britain by
Billings and Sons Limited, Worcester

INTRODUCTION

A. A. Thomson (Alex to friends) was a quiet man who wrote quietly and affectionately about cricket. Not for him the exaggerations of the livelier Press; not for him the keyhole discoveries so much in demand by some editors; not for him the revelations by players of dressing-room confidences uncovered more for cash than for credit. Thomson wrote about cricket for his own satisfaction and dignity. He never sought to hurt the game or its players.

Cricket writing was never his primary occupation. Had Hitler not interfered Thomson would probably have been a widely read novelist. He had just stepped on the literary ladder of that division when the war blocked his way. When publishing could be resumed with some freedom Thomson changed direction and, pleasing himself and pleasing others, he moved into the rising market of sports books in the 1950s. There he immediately found himself in a happy element. His early cricket books were readily acceptable to a readership eager to absorb pleasant writing in the nostalgic vein.

He wrote about the cricket he had seen and the cricket he had discovered in wide reading. He made no pretence of being a cricketer's cricketer. There is no evidence that he was a player of any substance and he certainly did not involve himself in the intricacies of cricketing technique. He sought neither to teach nor to preach. The flavour of cricket, the traditions of cricket and the personalities of cricket were his concern and abiding interest.

Most of the stories he told were acquired at second-hand. His skill was in selection and presentation of originality and wit. He did not attempt to say anything new or promulgate radical ideas. He watched, he remembered, and he recalled with obvious delight.

His early books became fashionable to the extent that at one time he was almost a cult in the critical columns. He was a fashionable and therefore successful cricket writer on the verge of cricket rather than in the middle of it. He had an eye for the unusual incident and character. In fact he made a collection of the unusual and titled it *Odd Men In*.

To Thomson the great cricketers of his own time and, indeed, their predecessors were painted larger than life. His favourites were all Olympians and often enough their slight imperfections were carefully overlooked. His nostalgic summers were all sunny and his batsmen and bowlers were always at the peak of their form.

Such a glow was, of course, difficult to preserve. Sometimes the figures tended to lose their earthy quality and become insubstantial representations without depth and balance. Just in time Thomson turned to more searching biography and produced, to my mind, the best of his work.

George Herbert Hirst and Wilfred Rhodes were ideal subjects. They were heroes of the first magnitude, heroes from his boyhood—where they glowed in imagination when his head was in the clouds, and became flesh and blood on the field before him when his feet were on the ground. They were wonderland heroes and the flesh and blood of his native environment. Thomson lived with Hirst and Rhodes in his daily thinking and breathing. Everyone in Yorkshire and in the rest of the cricketing world knew Hirst and Rhodes by name and reputation.

How much of Hirst and Rhodes Thomson saw on the fields he did not tell, but he knew enough to make their deeds unforgettable and their characters clear and coloured.

For his book Thomson was not in need of difficult research. All he wanted to know of their achievements was in the record books. The problem was of selectivity. Mere recital of their batting and bowling achievements would have been a catalogue piling wonder upon wonder to a point where the wondrous turned to commonplace. Thomson avoided the commonplace by retaining the peaks and clothing them in clouds of glory. All the romance Thomson sought could be found in unparalleled deeds. Who but Hirst ever scored 2,000 runs and took 200 wickets in one first-class season? Who but Rhodes ever held Test match records as a last-wicket batsman and a first-wicket batsman? Who but Hirst won match after match with astonishing batting and bowling for his native county? Who but

Rhodes played in his first Test match at the age of 21 and his last at the age of 51? From matters of fact they made miracles.

Thomson's biographies were no catalogues. The figures were not allowed to be more than the framework for his story. He used them as the canvas on which to paint pictures that appeared in three dimensions.

Thomson was carefully deliberate to keep his romantic notions under control. He avoided hyperbole without descending to the dull. He kept his decoration always to the point in his narrative. In *Hirst and Rhodes* Thomson brought his writing to the high level where art conceals art. You are enthralled by the story without appreciating how well and how lovingly that story is told.

He could present his characters in three-dimensional terms because he could feel the flesh and blood that made them living heroes. Hirst and Rhodes were professional cricketers who never assumed themselves any more or any less. They did not use cricket as a stepping-stone to a further career. They had no political, social or extraneous ambition beyond their choice of life and its fulfilment. Hirst and Rhodes were known the world over as cricketers and never thought of themselves by any other definition. Thomson therefore could tell a simple story of uncomplicated people in an uncomplicated existence. There were no secret papers to be revealed, no dark corners to be curtained off. Whatever Hirst and Rhodes did in cricket they did in the open field. They had nothing to hide, nothing to explain away.

Thomson took them as he and the rest of the cricketing world saw them. What he saw was good, the names were inevitably in association. Hirst and Rhodes bowled together, batted together, played together in perhaps the greatest of all county teams and they were together in what is usually regarded as the strongest England team ever to take the field. They were inevitably joined in the public mind and sometimes described as twin brothers in cricket. Here the public mind was mistaken and Thomson could mark the differences that were often overlooked in casual observations. Hirst and Rhodes were readily joined through their Yorkshire and Kirkheaton associations, but these incredible cricketers were many miles apart in their outlook and development and influence.

George Hirst was the extrovert. He played his cricket and

lived his life by the light of nature. He played day by day, taking what came with cheerful optimism and unshakeable belief in the rightness of things. He toiled, rejoiced and sorrowed according to the state of the game, never doubting clouds would break or right would triumph. He was an essential saviour of lost causes because he never considered them lost until the last run was scored or the last wicket taken. Then he put the day aside and looked forward happily to the next one. He played innings by innings, day by day and found happiness in everyone and everything, down to the pint and pipe that was his evening pleasure.

Rhodes took a longer view of circumstances. He played not in the hour alone but for the match and for the next match and for all the future. In his view a cricket career was a continuous experience. Today led to tomorrow, and yesterday was an entry in a professional notebook that could be re-opened whenever he chose. Roy Kilner said of Rhodes that when he had got you out once he had got you out twice because he knew how to do it again. Very few of the Rhodes achievements were attributable to chance or accident. All his accumulated wisdom was poured into every over he bowled. Rhodes did not discover his talent by accident. He considered what could be done, or might be done with a spinning ball and he confirmed the possibilities with chalk marks and unwearying patience. He played his cricket by scientific application and the closest observation of the conditions in which he was playing and the opponents he was challenging. Because of his own meticulous concern he was a hard taskmaster. When he set his field he expected his fieldsmen to accept his calculations. 'Always stay where you are put,' he insisted.

This book pays tribute to Hirst the happy cricketer, to Rhodes the one-man university of the game, and to A. A. Thomson who presented them with such pride.

Harrogate, 1985 J. M. Kilburn

A. A. THOMSON

****

Hirst and Rhodes

LONDON
THE EPWORTH PRESS

Author's Acknowledgement

MY sincere thanks for help and information are due to Miss Edna Denton, Miss Ann Hirst, and Mr Reginald Haigh and, more specifically, to H. S. Scales, L. E. S. Gutteridge; the President of the Huddersfield and District Cricket League, Herbert Robinson, and (as always) to cricket's great historian, H. S. Altham.

For their kindness in sending me reminiscences, pictures, and anecdotes I am also grateful to Messrs E. Norman Clark, Geoff Cocking, W. D. C. Denison, W. G. Evans, R. Haigh (of Scarborough), C. Hartley, S. McMillan, J. H. Nash, W. J. O'Reilly, P. Ll. Roberts, Peter Stone, Lieut.-Col. R. T. Stanyforth and Alderman Joe Thornton.

Contents

CHAPTER ONE

There were Giants

I

THERE were giants in the land in those days. True or false?
True: sometimes relatively and sometimes absolutely. In one
sense the legend is true in that the heroes of a man's boyhood
are for ever after twopence coloured and larger than life.
The soldiers, sailors, explorers, statesmen, and even villains
who appealed to the imagination of a schoolboy are likely to
retain their magnitude forty years on and it does not matter
when or where the boy went to school. No lad who ever
saw W. G. Grace's burly, bearded figure at the crease, small
bat clasped in mighty paws, was ever the same again, and
the young people, not necessarily all boys, who saw Jim
Laker take nineteen Australian wickets at Old Trafford in
1956, will bore their grandchildren with an expanding
narrative of the feat well into the next century. And justifi-
ably so. Breathes there a man with soul so dead that he will
not praise his own particular famous men?

These things, I say, are relative. Some men are heroes to
their own generation and that is just. But some men are
heroes to more than a generation. Others abide our question, they are free. Nelson was not merely a successful
admiral of the Regency period. Shakespeare was not merely
a popular plagiaristic playwright of an earlier Elizabethan
age. (I am assuming he wrote his own plays, because I think
he would have done the job better than the other candidates
for the post of authorship, singly or in relays.) Gladstone
was something more than a nineteenth-century Prime
Minister who consistently failed to amuse Queen Victoria.

Men of such high qualities as these were great by any standard in any generation.

Within the more modest ambit of cricket the same principles of the relative and the absolute hold good. Some cricketers are, or would have been, excellent in any age. Some, a select band, are built in such heroic mould and possess such heroic qualities that they transform their own time into a heroic age. Of this stature were George Herbert Hirst and Wilfred Rhodes, who so bore themselves that in their greatest days there blossomed around them a golden age of cricket in Yorkshire, and not only in Yorkshire, but in England.

II

If it is rash to describe the heyday of Hirst and Rhodes at the beginning of the century as *the* Golden Age, it would be absurd to deny that it was *a* golden age. Golden ages, in any event, are not all gold and do not last long. It can be maintained with some force that the present age is for cricket a golden one. Up to a point England could in the 1950s claim to possess the most powerful side put into the field for many, perhaps fifty, years. The only side to stand comparison with the England of 'my' Golden Age, other than the 1958-9 one, was the one that toured Australia under A. P. F. Chapman in 1928-9, but this splendid combination was numerically weak in bowling, though the bowlers, Tate, Larwood, White, and Geary, were individually magnificent and, in the event, wholly effective. But the England of 1958-9 was stronger; never, it could be argued, has a captain such a variety of good bowling at his command as Peter May had then. Were there ever at one time four fast bowlers so destructive —such unleashers of lightning—as Trueman, Statham, Loader, and Tyson? Or spin-bowlers of such varied guile as that remarkable pair, Laker and Lock? Here lay wealth indeed, and the fact that only four of this dominating half-dozen would normally be picked for one Test eleven seemed to show wealth to the point of embarrassment. Moreover, hardly any wicket-keeper of any age has come nearer to perfection in his difficult art than Godfrey Evans. The English spectator, mildly pessimistic at heart, asks for reliability and suspects brilliance in a wicket-keeper. But Evans's consistency has been so nearly flawless that his gaiety, his panache, his sheer quicksilver quality have been forgiven.

In batting, the excellence was not so well spread. Peter May certainly and Colin Cowdrey probably are of the stature of all but the very greatest giants of old. May has been a great batsman in a period when the bowler has been master. He is young yet and has, I believe, the career of a Hobbs or a Bradman before him. No one who saw May and Cowdrey bat in the Birmingham Test of 1957 can think of those two young men without a lift of the heart. But after May and Cowdrey the gap between the great and the good —even the very good, like the brilliant Graveney and Peter Richardson, is hard to bridge. Even so, it was hard to deny that bowlers, backed by relentless fielding, won matches; what seemed to be required was not a glittering array of master-batsmen, but the minimum of workmanlike skill at the crease needed to make the runs, once the bowlers had done their destructive work. This is a modern theory and there is some force, if little beauty, in it.

Indeed, a county captain not so long ago jocularly confessed to me the secret of his team's single success in the Championship. 'Bad batting,' he said, 'and never winning the toss.' By this he meant, I take it, that his bowlers were never handicapped by having to get their opponents out twice in a time made too short, because their batsmen had batted too long. There is, I repeat, a good deal in this theory, and Surrey, not England's stoutest batting side, though carrying England's one unchallengeably great batsman, have thriven exceedingly on it. But it can go wrong.

For what happens if a team produces all-rounders, as it might be Benaud and Davidson, who can bowl as effectively as your specialist bowlers and bat rather better than your batsman? The fact is that, however well your specialist bowlers may serve you, there comes a time when they must be supported by sounder batting. The lack of this is an Achilles heel and if you can only bat down to No. 6, your Achilles heel reaches up to the small of your back. This is the time you need a Hirst and a Rhodes.

III

It is interesting to compare the powerful, if vulnerable, team of today with one from the day before yesterday, say, the 1902 eleven that outplayed the Australians at Birmingham and were only robbed by rain of overwhelming victory. The side batted in this order: A. C. MacLaren, C. B. Fry, Tyldesley, K. S. Ranjitsinhji, Braund, Hon. F. S. Jackson, G. L. Jessop, Hirst, Lilley, Lockwood, and Rhodes. If you are sixty years old these names will ring out in your ears like trumpet calls; they are the epic muster-roll of authentic gods and heroes. If you are somewhat younger you may feel that these old fellows were all very well till Hobbs and Hammond came along, and if you are much younger you will wonder what all the fuss was about, anyway.

Yet consider the sheer aristocracy of this eleven. At No. 1 is the majestic A. C. MacLaren, whom Neville Cardus called 'the noblest Roman of them all'. At No. 2 is C. B. Fry, the greatest all-round athlete of his own, or, all things considered, any age; a classical scholar and a triple Blue at Oxford, who the year before had scored six successive centuries, a feat never surpassed and only equalled by Sir Donald Bradman. At No. 4 came Ranji, to whom the over-used adjective 'legendary' can be applied without outrage, because he became a legend early in his lifetime, an Oriental magician whose strokes were as swift, delicate, and deadly as the sweep of a scimitar; and at No. 7 was Jessop, an equally vivid and fantastic figure, a batsman so ruthless in his controlled hitting that, more than any other player, he could, by his very presence and off his own bat, swing the game round to triumph from disaster, as indeed he did, in the fifth Test of that series which will for ever be known as Jessop's match. And at No. 3. the post of highest honour, stands Johnny Tyldesley, a russet-coated captain among these plumed cavaliers, deemed worthy of such peerless companions and accepted by them as an equal, the only professional batsman in a batting array jewelled with brilliant amateurs.

The wicket-keeper was Arthur Augustus (Dick) Lilley, not as dazzling to the eye as Gregor McGregor who came before or Godfrey Evans who came afterwards, but the very acme of soundness. Lilley wore England's stumping-gloves for nearly twenty years, and his right to them was never questioned. At this point, with five superlative batsmen and the most dependable of wicket-keepers, a modern selection committee would proceed to pick, if they had not already done so, five specialist bowlers, hardly one of whom could be guaranteed to score ten runs in a crisis. In the 1902 eleven there were no specialist bowlers, unless you counted young Wilfred Rhodes, who ten years later was to go in first instead of last for England and to pile up a first-wicket partnership record that was to last for over thirty years.

The strength of that eleven lay in its all-rounders, that type of player who has given so much high quality to his side and so much pleasure to spectators; who could, by an individual effort of either batting or bowling, turn the tide of a game from defeat to victory. Since the second World War all-rounders in England have been rare. In the other countries of the Commonwealth, men like Keith Miller, Mankad, Trevor Goddard, Worrell, Benaud, Davidson, and Sobers have not been quite so hard to find. Today in

England there is only Trevor Bailey, for whose talents as batsman, bowler, fielder, and fighter I have a respect bordering on awe; indeed, I have often thought that the best contemporary England eleven obtainable would consist of a wicket-keeper, four batsmen, four bowlers and two Baileys. For the modern sin of slow play Bailey has unjustly been made the scapegoat. Within the restricted area of the contemporary game Bailey has only followed the path of duty. The evil lies in the inflation of Test match time from three to five and six days. This carries with it the inexorable fulfilment of Parkinson's Law: *Work expands so as to fill the time available for its completion.* So do not blame Bailey, England's one all-rounder. But while today Bailey is England's one ewe-lamb, the 1902 fold contained a whole flock. There was Braund, a Surrey migrant to Somerset, a leg-spinner who had once bowled fast, a punishing opening bat for his county, and a darting, dazzling slip-field, the most illustrious before Hammond. There was F. S. Jackson, an orthodox batsman who hit harder and an orthodox medium-fast bowler who bowled straighter than most of either kind, a fighter with a flair for victory. (Three years later he captained England against the next visiting Australians, won the toss five times, headed both batting and bowling averages for the series and retained the Ashes for England with the highest personal honours.) Jessop was not only the hurricane hitter of the side but was also a fast bowler of high merit, capable of working up a devastating speed in his first few overs. If Lockwood seemed a little nearer to being a specialist bowler than the other all-rounders in the England eleven, he was with his county a sound hard-hitting batsman who had made many good scores at the Oval. In the last match of the 1902 series—Jessops's match —he played an absolutely vital part in the stand with Hirst for the ninth wicket which saved the follow-on and made victory possible.

And finally there were Hirst and Rhodes. As a small boy I worshipped Hirst and Rhodes as I worshipped Dickens. Those three were the most wonderful things that happened in my life.

IV

The era of Hirst and Rhodes, if you reckon it from the time when Hirst received his first trial for the county to the end of the season when Rhodes finally retired from the first-class game, is all of forty-one years. Whichever way you look at it, their cricketing lives and cricketing genius lie at the heart of cricket's history, but let us for a moment narrow it down to the period at the beginning of the century, when their county reigned supreme. There were giants in England and giants in Yorkshire.

The county team of 1900, 1901, and 1902, which won the championship three years in succession with only two defeats (both at the eager hands of Somerset) could claim almost the same quality and stature as the England elevens of the same period. In 1900 they went through their programme with sixteen victories and no defeats, and their draws were due to poor weather and not to pusillanimous tactics. No county side had gone through a season undefeated since the competition had become a real one. They themselves would have modestly said that they would have done better, only they could never place their best eleven in the field because F. S. Jackson, Frank Mitchell, and F. W. Milligan were fighting in South Africa, and the last of these, a talented player and a much-loved person, died there. Yet the Yorkshire side was strong enough to beat off all comers, and Lancashire, their nearest rivals, finished with one fewer victory and some defeats.

Look at the bowlers first, for in Yorkshire bowling is the bread-and-butter of cricket; batting is only the jam. The leading bowlers of that year were Rhodes, who took 240 wickets at a cost of less than 13 runs apiece, and Haigh, the

17

third member of a valiant triumvirate, who took 160 for 14 runs each. Oddly enough, in 1900 Hirst was for once no champion with the ball; he took only fifty-odd wickets that season, leaving it till the next to raise the number to 171.

A typical eleven of the period would be: Brown, Tunnicliffe, Denton, T. L. Taylor, Hirst, Wainwright, Lees Whitehead, Haigh, Lord Hawke, Rhodes, and Hunter. In August a place would be found for Ernest Smith, one of that noble army of schoolmasters who, the moment they have signed their last term report, pack their long cricket bags and dash away to the north, south, east or west, in whichever direction their counties need strengthening.

Brown and Tunnicliffe formed the second of those powerful first-wicket pairs—Ulyett and Hall, Rhodes and B. B. Wilson, Holmes and Sutcliffe, Sutcliffe and Hutton—which have for long periods made Yorkshire's batting almost as wholesomely feared as their bowling. I have little doubt that the Holmes-Sutcliffe axis was the most formidable of these, but J. T. Brown and John Tunnicliffe broke the ground and paved the way for it. The two were nicely contrasted, as is the way with great pairs: Brown was a stylist and elegant late-cutter, hero of at least one tremendous Test match with A. E. Stoddart's 1894-5 team in Australia. Tunnicliffe—Long John—was the first of that happy band of pilgrims who began life's pilgrimage from Pudsey. That town's *sobriquet*, Pearl of the West Riding, may be a tribute to its inhabitants' imagination, but Pudsey has certainly produced cricketers who have made the world their oyster: Tunnicliffe, Major Booth (who died gallantly in the 1914-18 war), the immaculate, imperturbable Herbert Sutcliffe; Sir Leonard Hutton, who was the greatest batsman of his day, solid Harry Halliday, and one of the most promising of today's all-rounders, Raymond Illingworth.[1] Tunnicliffe, tall,

[1] The world is full enough of trouble without starting a cold war as to where Farsley ends and Pudsey begins. They are near enough.

serious-minded, and his captain's most trusted professional lieutenant until Hirst graduated to that post, was the 'straight' man of the opening partnership, defending steadfastly while Brown batted with grace and daring. He probably covered more ground with his firm-footed forward defensive stroke than any other batsman. If any slip-fielder of that generation had a higher reputation than Tunnicliffe it was the England player Braund and Braund only, but, if Braund was more brilliant, Tunnicliffe took more catches. His anticipation was equally uncanny and his immense length of limb often saved him the trouble of emulating Braund's footwork. Yorkshire people said that catches just hung on him like hats on a hat-rack. And, just as Louis Hall (opening bat and 'Prince of Stonewallers') had been, he was an active lay member of the Methodist Church. In every sense he was a steadying influence.

The third member of Yorkshire's first trio was David Denton, called, perhaps unluckily, Lucky Denton, because fielding captains were alleged to say as he approached the crease: 'Come on, lads, who's going to miss him first?' Denton, with his cavalry moustache of the period and his quick-footed spirit of attack which always made his bat seem like a darting weapon, was the nearest thing to a *beau sabreur* Yorkshire ever produced. He was incapable of dullness. You could get him out (though this was extremely difficult on his day), but you could not tie him up. When he retired and for a time became a first-class umpire, he is reported to have said: 'You know, there's one thing I've learnt for the first time at this job: a no-ball counts one.' When Denton batted, the only time a no-ball did not count four was when it counted six. Denton competed with Hirst over a slightly later period for the reputation of being Yorkshire's most prolific batsman and, in any season, the gay fury of his onslaught on the bowling was more than compensation for his occasional inconsistency. If he had fewer England caps than he deserved, it was because his country's No. 3 position was superlatively held by J. T. Tyldesley. If you were the next best to Tyldesley, you were very good indeed. It has always been the habit of Yorkshire players at Scarborough's end-of-season festival to relax from the grimmer labours of the championship, but it was said of Denton that 'he was playing at Scarborough all the time'. Moreover, he was a sure-handed, swift-footed long-fieldsman, the best of his day—a day when many a batsman regarded valour as the better part of discretion and would rather drive a ball into the long-field than tickle it round the corner.

The fourth man in the usual batting order was T. L. Taylor, who, with Rhodes, is one of the two survivors from Yorkshire's greater days, and a vigorous survivor at that. Now he is president of the county club; then he was captain of Cambridge, and four years before that he had been captain of Uppingham and the outstanding public-school batsman of the year. He had unyielding powers of concentration, enjoyed battling it out with the bowlers on a bad wicket and, always excepting Hirst, was Yorkshire's most obstinate back-to-the-wall fighter in moments of crisis. *Wisden's* chapter describing the five chosen Cricketers of the Year—that is, of 1900—is headed 'Mr R. E. Foster and Four Yorkshiremen'. The four were T. L. Taylor, Tunnicliffe, Hirst, and Haigh, and Taylor's place in such illustrious company was richly deserved.

Ted Wainwright, by 1900 well advanced in his career, was another of those Yorkshire all-rounders who, though not outstanding to the same degree as Hirst, Rhodes, and Jackson, have been valuable members of the eleven, always pulling their weight and a little bit more and capable of rising grandly to the awkward occasion. The season of 1900 was not one of Wainwright's brightest, but in the Roses match at Old Trafford, with the current flowing strongly against Yorkshire, he stood in the breach and 'dammed the flowing tide' with a fifty that was worth more than many a hundred obtained in easier circumstances. Ted, an off-spinner who could really turn the ball, was a bit of a character, even for a Yorkshireman, and must have caused his captain one or two frowns, but when this happened he could usually whip out some amusing answer to unfurrow even the baronial brow.

Schofield Haigh was the third member of a mighty trio: Hirst, Rhodes, and Haigh; in any other triumvirate, he would have been the first. It is impossible to praise Hirst and Rhodes too much, but it is possible to praise Haigh too little. He was a lovable personality, an incorrigible practical joker, and a very fine player indeed. If not such a complete all-rounder as the other two, he was a medium-paced bowler of the utmost menace, who was content with a fairly modest position in the batting order, but could time after time pull out a defiant innings at need. He had a fierce individual talent for bowling just outside the off-stump a ball which would venomously break-back the width of the wicket to knock the leg-stump out of the ground. It seemed as though he deprecated the fieldsman's aid and preferred to dispatch his victims single-handed. If you look down a match-score of the period you will see the phrase, *b. Haigh, b. Haigh, b. Haigh*, repeating itself in a pleasing if slightly monotonous pattern, looking a bit like free verse, but aesthetically and intellectually more pleasing. At least three of his observations have passed into Yorkshire folklore. These were: (1) his reply to the wicket-keeper who classed him among the rabbits: 'I've got the key of the hutch!'; (2) his verdict, following the inspection of a sticky pitch: 'Methinks they'll deviate somewhat'; and (3) his agonized oration at a presentation dinner, which consisted of the repetition, at increasing intervals for meditation, of the deathless phrase: 'Well, I'm glad we've won t'Cup!' Folklore indeed. Well did Old Ebor, Yorkshire's most revered chronicler, name him as 'for eighteen years the sunshine of the Yorkshire eleven'.

David Hunter, that shrewd, quiet-voiced wicketkeeper, who lived in Scarborough and kept canaries, suffered in one respect as Denton, the other David, suffered. Just as Denton over the relevant period was slightly overshadowed by Tyldesley, so was Hunter slightly overshadowed by Lilley. It is hard to be second best, especially by so small a margin, but Hunter lived a contented life, crafty as a stumper, friendly as a man.

Lord Hawke's captaincy probably represents history's only genuine example of a benevolent autocracy, if only because autocracies are not by nature benevolent. As for this particular autocrat, his benevolence was unchallenged and his autocracy has been wildly exaggerated. The picture of him painted by some modern journalists as an arrogant peer (out of the chorus of *Iolanthe*), spurning with his cane a mob of ragged, trembling serfs labelled cricket professionals, is as false as it is ludicrous. When he took over the captaincy, he found himself in charge of a body of talented, hearty, and unruly buccaneers; when he retired he left as splendidly welded a county side as ever took the field, and, throughout that time, he was more benevolent and less autocratic than Brian Sellers, Yorkshire's other great captain, could begin to be. Whatever Lord Hawke may have said on the possibility of professional captaincy—and what he said has been sub-jected to more distortion and misrepresentation than the Zinoviev letter—he was without question the best friend the professional cricketer of the day ever had. Individual standards of pay, security, and status were immeasurably improved under his leadership, and more than one old pro. spent a comfortable old age because of Lord Hawke's insistence that benefit money should be safeguarded. He was, furthermore, not merely his professionals' mentor, but a skilful strategist on the field and a reputable batsman who deserved a higher place in the order than the No. 9 at which he normally placed himself. (In Yorkshire's record score of 887 he made 166.) Times have changed and many of the forms of cricket have changed with them. Now the notion of a kindly martinet as county captain no longer fits into the social picture, and it would be churlish to grudge the skilled and likeable young professional cricketers of today their privileges. Yet if they enjoy a fuller and freer life than their fathers and grandfathers, they owe more than they know to Lord Hawke.

Two members of this classic Yorkshire eleven have yet to have individual mention. Their names are Hirst and Rhodes.

CHAPTER TWO

Kirkheaton Lad

'He at once sent out a flavour of nature, broad, homely, humorous, fine. . . . As a cricketer he came straight down from Hambledon and the pastures.'—Neville Cardus

I

IT IS AN ancient joke, greatly venerated, as are all ancient traditions in the Huddersfield district, that nobody knows the name of the world's greatest all-round cricketer. All we know for certain is that he batted right-hand, bowled left and was born in Kirkheaton. Now Kirkheaton is a small stone-built village, firmly dug in—nestling would be out of character—on the slopes of the Pennines and there George Herbert Hirst was born in 1871 and Wilfred Rhodes in 1877. As for who was the greatest of all-round cricketers Hirst said, characteristically, that it was Rhodes, and Rhodes, also characteristically, has always declined to say.

So we are left with Kirkheaton and its wind-swept cricket field where young George Hirst first saw bat and ball. The Kirkheaton Cricket Club belongs to the Huddersfield and District League, which, with the possible exception of the Bradford League, is probably the most zealous cricket league in the country. I spent a pleasant afternoon ambling through the village and then watching a keen League game on the cricket ground. I saw the original site of the Brown Cow where George Herbert was born and which has been pulled down in the interest of road improvement. 'It was the first place of call,' I was solemnly told, 'when folk went off on their char-a-banc outings.' On the other side of the road was a row of cottages built of the grey Yorkshire stone known

24

as Crosland Hall stone and planned in the same style as the
Brown Cow had been; in the deep dip below the road,
pleasantly known as t'Bottom, lies the field that was once
the old cricket ground. (There is a still older field higher up
the slope, where the boys played in the 1870s, which is still
known as the Moor.) There is a fine old church whose yard
contains two curious monuments. One is the headstone, show-
ing bat, ball, and broken wicket, of Andrew Greenwood,
one of the five Yorkshiremen who took part in the first of all
Test matches, played at Melbourne in 1877. The other is an
obelisk which commemorates the dreadful fate of seventeen
child workers who were burnt to death in a nearby factory
fire in 1818. It was this hideous tragedy which drove the
famous Richard Oastler into his inspired lifelong campaign
for factory reform.

Above the village the present-day cricket ground, which
was founded in 1883, lies on a high wide shelf, set among the
hills and flanked by a drystone wall. A Kirkheaton man will
stand by the pavilion and point with a sweep of his arm all
round the points of the compass. 'There's Wakefield,' he
will say, 'there's Barnsley, there's Bradford. . . .' But you
will not see these places, only the direction in which they lie.
You will see an undulating line of green hills, two television
masts, the smoke of Huddersfield's chimneys, and, directly
across the lovely valley, white-clad cricketers playing on the
Lascelles Hall ground. The drystone wall that surrounds the
great trim circle of the Kirkheaton ground gives welcome
shelter from winds which up there can sometimes wuther
without mercy.

The playing surface is shallow; between the level, green
turf and the hard rock underneath there is no more than a
foot of earth. There are two pavilions: the old one with its
high scoring-box has something of the air of a compressed
Noah's ark; the other has a magic name, for it is called the
'Hirst and Rhodes'. It was built with the stones from a

disused chapel and its foundations were officially laid on
26th August 1950 by the great men themselves. Sitting on
the bench in front of the pavilion's wire-guarded windows
were two or three of Hirst's old cronies of far-off days.

'Ay,' said First Crony, 'you can see the two foundation
stones and both of 'em'—a chuckle ran solemnly along the
bench—'both of 'em was laid by *left-handed bricklayers*.' Then
solemnly we turned our attention to the cricket being played
in front of us.

If the people of Kirkheaton are keen on cricket now, their
ardour was even warmer in George Hirst's young days. They
ate, drank, and dreamed cricket; and their womenfolk
brought them tea to the old pavilion between innings and
called it, as they still call it, the 'tea tent'. The ladies of
Kirkheaton still carry on this noble work. Ministering angels
also ran. On Saturday evenings the cricketers fought their
battles over again in the bar-parlour of the Brown Cow, and
on Sunday mornings, on the way home from church or
chapel, they would illustrate winning or disastrous strokes
with their umbrellas. Young George was playing regularly
for the village side by the time he was fifteen, and when one
of the Sunday papers offered prizes for outstanding performances by club cricketers he was instantly conspicuous.

'One week it would be for bowling,' said one of the
Cronies, 'and another week it would be for batting, but
George Herbert earned every prize that was going, even if
he didn't get 'em.'

It was always 'George Herbert', never just 'George' with
the Cronies. By the double name they seemed to imply an
additional affection and respect. In the old days Hirst,
Rhodes, and Schofield Haigh would come up for practice
long before the season started, sometimes as early as Pancake
Tuesday. They were 'tremendous practisers', said one of
the Cronies, and Mrs Schofield Haigh would come with
them. She was a real Trojan. If it was too wet for bat and

ball they would have a go with knurr and spell. George
Hirst himself once told me that practice was a serious
business. 'When I was a lad at Kirkheaton,' he said, 'we
took the side-nets away and every ball had to be fielded.'
Schofield Haigh was the champion joker of the trio, but if
he pulled your leg too hard, George Herbert would say:
'Talk back at him, talk back at him!'

Though naturally Hirst developed in strength of body and
mind as he came to manhood, he retained throughout his life
much of the spirit of that Kirkheaton lad: sturdiness, good
temper, and a wholehearted determination to use bat, ball,
and his capacious pair of hands to the greatest advantage and
to fight his side's way out of trouble. Though I had seen him
on the field since my own boyhood, I did not meet him
personally till he was over seventy. In his manner then he
showed a kind of mellow gentleness, not usually associated
with eminent fast bowlers, but a reminder of his sturdiness,
of his genial strength, and of a still excited love of the game
remained with him, and would remain till he died.

When George Herbert left school (and he left at the
age of ten) he was employed as a wirer for a hand-loom
weaver, working in a corner cottage at the bottom of the road
that rises steeply toward Lascelles Hall. After that he worked
in Robson's dye-works on the other side of the valley, and all
the time he was playing cricket as a 'Saturday man', first for
Elland, then for Mirfield, and afterwards for Huddersfield.
In the winter he played Rugby football and it would have
been hard to find a sturdier full-back.

When he first had a trial for Yorkshire at the age of
eighteen, his equipment only slightly resembled that of his
humorous and exuberant predecessor, Tom Emmett from
Halifax, who to his first professional engagement at half a
crown a match carried his equipment in a copy of the local
paper and walked to the field in clogs.

'I was different,' George Hirst recalled. 'My gear was

worth all of ten shillings and I carried it in a canvas bag.
I wore a shilling cap, a sixpenny belt with a snake-clasp and
brown boots. At the trial I bowled in my sweater, but I was
better off than Arthur Mold of Lancashire, who couldn't
take his off because he had no shirt on underneath. My
shirt was blue but I got a white one with my first money. . . .'

ii

His first trial for the county took place in 1889[1] and he was not
given another real game for two years, when he took a couple
of wickets against Somerset and scored only 15 runs. He
was called on a few more times in 1892 and did considerably
better, but it was in the following year, Yorkshire's first true
championship season, that he began building a name for
himself. He was already bowling with much of the wholeheartedness, though with less of the skill, that he was to
display in later, richer years. He was (Lord Hawke said) 'a
young bowler with a nice action, straight and quick'. He was
sending down fastish left-hand straight stuff which, as the
season went on, disturbed an increasing number of wickets,
and by the time September came along he had claimed 99.
In 1893 Yorkshire's best bowlers were, according to the
record, Peel, Wainwright, and this comparative newcomer
Hirst. *Wisden* said of the third of these that he maintained
his form and 'strengthened the good impression he had
made'. The impression he made as a batsman was not quite
so strong and, despite the quickness of his eye and footwork,
he was still kept down in the lowly position of No. 10. All
the same, he made some useful scores, and a hard-hit 35 not
out in a low-scoring match at Huddersfield against Gloucestershire made W. G. Grace give an appreciative tug at his
beard. Hirst's batting was immature, but it had the basic
elements of future power and all his lusty youthful strength
went into his pulling and hooking.

[1] The scorers even spelt his name wrong.

'Ha,' said W. G. wryly, 'I'd no idea the beggar could bat, too.'

III

In 1894 he strengthened his position as a worthwhile member of the side. His bowling was of much the same robust quality as before, and he was credited with only one wicket fewer, thus barely missing the hundred for the second year in succession. His batting, following W. G.'s commendation, grew at the same time more watchful and more punitive, and, just to remind the Old Man of his existence, he hit a not out 100 against Gloucestershire which contained seventeen fours. But it was not so much any particular performance that won his county's increased respect as his natural aptitude in a tight corner. 'Repeatedly', says the chronicler, 'he came to the rescue of his side when things were going badly.' His motto might well have been: 'Once more unto the breach.' This appetite for heavy rescue work was in time to become almost a form of gluttony and, from this year onward, he turned himself into a kind of cricketing Horatius, holding his county's bridges, however fierce the onslaught.

It was in 1895 that for the first time he secured 100 wickets, carrying his season's total up to 150, making sure that there should be no mistake. He had not yet made a thousand runs in a season, but each summer was bringing him nearer, and 710 looked a nice round figure, even though so far it was only as a bowler that he had been taken seriously. For the first time he was more effective than Wainwright in opening the bowling, especially with Peel as a partner at the other end. Those were the days before the policy of beginning the attack with two fast bowlers became a slavishly worshipped fetish; a captain would often begin his attack with one fast bowler and one slow one. Thus Hirst and Peel were frequently used in combination, and some seasons later Hirst and Rhodes became the most formidable of all bowling

29

pairs. The vigour of Hirst's onset was not confined to any one kind of wicket. Wet or dry, sticky or plumb, it mattered little to him, for he attacked with tireless energy, literally hurling himself into the work with the queer hop, step, and jump of his initial run. The batsmen of that year's Middlesex eleven had reason to remember him, for he captured twelve of their wickets at Leeds. Earlier in a successful Roses game at Bramall Lane he took five for 63. To do well in this match was the hallmark of a fighter, for between Yorkshire and Lancashire no quarter was asked or given.

The next year saw Yorkshire's second championship and the first of Hirst's fourteen 'doubles', which comprised 1,122 runs and 104 wickets. For the first time the wiseacres began to shake their heads warningly. Was this lad not paying too much attention to the meretricious arts of batting? After all, bowling was what they played him for. This complaint was something different from the present-day distrust of all-rounders as such. In the northern counties there has always been a strong feeling that bowling matters most and that batting exists only to make certain that the real work of the bowlers is not wasted. The critics need not have worried quite so much. They might at least have remembered the all-round excellence of Yorkshiremen like Tom Emmett and George Ulyett, each of whom had given his best to batting or to bowling, whichever was needed most at the time. But they did not know enough to look forward to a time when this youngster would bat and bowl with a bounding and boundless vigour never seen on the cricket field before.

Several years were to pass before his well-wishers finally gave up saying: 'He'll have to make up his mind whether he means to bowl or bat.'

IV

They did not say it so loudly in the Golden Jubilee year of 1897, because his accomplishments were nicely balanced.

His total of 1,535 runs was his highest so far and he secured his 100 wickets, even if it took him to the end of the season to make certain of it. Yorkshire, who fell to fourth place in the championship, had some exciting matches, which included their defeat at the hands of Essex at Huddersfield by one run and a crushing rout from Gloucestershire at Harrogate. In this game Jessop set off one of his fantastic firework displays, scoring 101 out of 118 in forty minutes, smashing the pavilion clock and putting one six through the roof of a cab outside the ground. The horse bolted and did not stop running till arrested in the city of Leeds, fifteen miles away. Or so they will tell you. Both as friends and foes, Hirst and Jessop were to write epoch-making pages in cricket history.

Yorkshire's hardest-fought victory was won over Derbyshire at Derby. Left with 154 to make in the fourth innings, they did not seem to have an insurmountable task, but F. S. Jackson and Brown were dismissed for a couple of runs and things went on running badly until Hirst came in at No. 7. After that, though the newcomer stood as firm as a rock, matters went from bad to worse. Hirst farmed the bowling with the utmost courage and skill, but every time the bowlers were allowed a glimpse of his vulnerable partners, another wicket fell. By the time the ninth broken reed had gone, Hirst had scored 49 heroic runs, but 16 were still needed. The last man in was David Hunter, most reliable of wicket-keepers but frankly no master-batsman, and the prospect of a Derbyshire victory loomed visibly—to Derbyshire's excited supporters. To beat Yorkshire was for many the dream of a lifetime, a dream whose realization required to be celebrated in the grand manner. As David Hunter came stumping down the pavilion steps, he heard the Derbyshire secretary say to the dressing-room attendant: 'Bring out the champagne, Harry.' This was a natural request, but for David Hunter it was an insult to his capacity as a batsman. Out to the wicket he strode, darkly muttering: 'I'll give 'em champagne!'

There was one ball of the over left; if Hunter could only survive this one ball, then Hirst at the other end, well set for his fifty and brimming with fighting confidence, might still have a chance to pull the game out of the fire. To the dismay of every Yorkshireman on the ground, Hunter boldly hit the ball in front of the wicket, called for a run and, against all the strategic rules, charged purposefully to the other end. Hirst would have sent him back, but there was no time and so he had to scramble across himself. Hunter, who now had to face the bowling, had committed an act of insensate folly. Could he live through another ball, never mind another over? Several of the Yorkshire players in the pavilion looked the other way. Off the first ball he hit a four; off the second another four; off the third, a third; the fourth ball he hit far away on the leg side and the batsmen ran for their lives. Whether the ball reached the boundary or not, no one ever knew, for as they finished their third run, the match was won and the spectators were hysterically scrambling on to the playing area. As the two batsmen forced their way back through the crowd, Hunter's face still did not relax.

'Champagne,' he muttered. 'I said I'd show 'em!'

And George Hirst had been robbed of his nobly earned fifty.

CHAPTER THREE

Towards Greatness

'A great "natural" genius, frank and open, yet blending
scientific orthodoxy with primitive skill.'—A. E. Knight

I

A. E. STODDART's team which toured Australia in 1897-8
contained two Yorkshiremen; one was Ted Wainwright, who
had just completed his finest season. The second was
George Hirst.

Three years before, Stoddart had taken a side to Australia
and succeeded splendidly. Everything they did went right.
With the 1897-8 tourists almost everything went wrong. On
paper they were a shining company and almost every
member of the side at one time or another did brilliant
things, but after a scintillating start in the first Test, they
seemed, as a team, to fall to pieces. There was a good deal
of sickness, a heavier crop of injuries than usual, and, worst
of all, an unaccountable loss of form in all the bowlers
except J. T. Hearne. The beautiful billiard-table wickets of
Australia were peculiarly hard on the English bowlers,
especially the two Yorkshiremen. Wainwright, fresh from
all-round successes at home and master of a colossal off-break,
could not make the ball turn at all. (When he got home, he
went straight to the nets at Bramall Lane and, without taking
his coat off, he bowled the ball that the Australian pitches
had anaesthetized. 'It broke a foot,' said honest Ted, 'and
I nearly jumped over t'moon!') Hirst, hampered by a
strained leg, batted unevenly and bowled without his usual
penetration. He was not, of course, a complete failure: he
had valuable scores of 62 in the first Test and 85 in the

second; moreover, he hit up some merry scores in less vital matches. But his bowling figures told a sad story, lamentably prophetic of Mr J. J. Warr's one for 281 half a century later.

Hirst's misfortunes of strained leg, loss of form, and sheer fatigue dogged him through the season that followed at home. Though one of the physically strongest and most enthusiastic cricketers who ever played anywhere, he took a long time to throw off the effects of that first Australian tour. His second tour, six years later, was wholly free from unhappy results and the season that followed it was one of his best and most vigorous. As it turned out, the season of 1898 was the only one of his playing career which could be described as 'bad for Hirst, but good for Yorkshire'.

One reason why Yorkshire did not suffer more severely from the temporary eclipse of their most energetic all-rounder was that they had been lucky enough to discover the young bowler who was in time to become the only cricketer who could possibly be considered a greater all-rounder than his friend and neighbour. The newcomer was Wilfred Rhodes, another Kirkheaton lad, and the two of them were henceforth to be immortally linked as no cricketers had been before, not even 'my Hornby and my Barlow long ago . . .'. In his first season Rhodes took 154 wickets and was honoured in *Wisden* as one of the five Cricketers of the Year. Nothing like this first-season success was achieved by any bowler of any county until fifty-three years later.

II

For more than twenty years Hirst and Rhodes were to be the greatest pair on the field. Without either or both of them cricket would have been a poorer, duller game. But in the first place Hirst had to recover from the setback in form and fitness that he had suffered in the season of 1898, and this in 1899 he proceeded to do, rising from what were, for him at least, abysmal depths to the highly respectable achievement of 1,630 runs, including three successive centuries, at an average of 35, and 82 wickets at a cost of less than 25 runs apiece. It was not a double, but it was something creditably near it and contained, as had almost every season's record, some valiant performances with both bat and ball. He had the distinction of playing in his first home Test match in that unlucky game at Nottingham which was to be W. G.'s last. Hirst did nothing as batsman or bowler to justify the selectors' faith in him; in fact, it was argued that he only found a place in the eleven as a fourth choice, because Lockwood, Bradley, and Kortright were injured or out of form. In his one innings he made six and took one wicket for 62, but *Wisden* praised his fielding at mid-off as brilliant, saying that he was almost entitled to be picked on that alone. I can only think of Jessop of whom the same could have been said. In an article written for the sole purpose of castigating the slackness of contemporary fielding, D. L. A. Jephson cited Hirst as one of half a dozen honourable exceptions to an unworthy rule: 'You may as well drive through a brick wall as try to pass those iron hands.'

CHAPTER FOUR

The Mighty Years

'When you think of cricket as a game, George Hirst is the ideal cricketer.'—A. E. Knight

I

ALL THESE years, it seemed, Hirst had been building up his energies for 1900, the first year of Yorkshire's great triennium. These were the years in which the Yorkshire eleven, once regarded as a collection of brilliant but erratic individualists, were beginning to establish themselves as a superlatively powerful combination, armed at all points against all possible opponents on all kinds of wickets. Once they had been a company of irregulars. Now they were a regiment, superbly accoutred and well tempered in discipline. They remained a great bowling side rather than a great batting side, for that is, as we have seen, the north country way. Thus Yorkshire could win their matches when Sussex, led by such fantastically prolific run-getters as Fry and Ranjitsinhji, could only draw the greater part of theirs. In 1901 Yorkshire won 20 out of their 27 matches and lost only one. (This was the game at Headingley in which they were sensationally—and for once the adverb is rightly used—routed by Somerset.) Fry and Ranji towered almost arrogantly over the country's batting averages with 78 and 70, and rarely can batsmen of any age have shown such consistent mastery. Yet the factor that counted even more was the work of the two men who stood as the top of the first-class bowling tables. These were Rhodes (251 at 15·12) and Hirst (183 at 16·38). This was the first of Hirst's 'great' years. He had achieved the double twice before and was to

repeat the feat eleven times in the next twelve years. His
greatest year was to be 1906, a season which brought him the
unparalleled figures of over 2,000 runs and 200 wickets.
His splendid work in 1901 gave the first true foretaste of this
tremendous achievement.

His success in bowling was due to his development, for the
first time seriously, of his remarkable ability to make the ball
swerve in the air. This swerve was almost as revolutionary
as the googly that B. J. T. Bosanquet was to use three years
later. Today scientists could demonstrate exactly how Hirst
achieved his swerve, and other scientists, equally dogmatic,
would prove that it was physically impossible for him to have
made the ball swerve as fiercely as batsmen said he did.
Hirst himself, as always, said little and, when questioned,
was uniformly modest about this rather unaccountable
attainment. 'Sometimes it works,' he said, 'and sometimes
it doesn't.' He was essentially modest because he was
essentially honest. As with some of his other outstanding
feats, he knew that he could not do the trick in every game,
and that he could not keep up the particular pressure
throughout a very long innings. Yet while the spell lasted,
the most technically gifted batsmen were reduced to im-
potence and could make no more of this queer business than
their own tail-enders. Hirst's full destructive power was
dependent on the state, not of the wicket, but of the atmosphere. With a head-wind, rather than a cross-wind, blow-
ing, the 'unnatural' behaviour of the ball was bewildering
and a bemused S. M. J. (Sammy) Woods expressed the
feelings of many when he demanded: 'How the devil can
you play a ball that comes in at you like a hard throw-in
from cover-point?' By any standard Hirst's best performances of 1901 are immensely impressive: 5 for 11 against
Sussex; seven for 21 against Leicestershire; seven for 23 in
a Roses match at Old Trafford; seven for 24 against Kent,
and six for 26 against Notts. Even out of this catalogue of

semi-miraculous deeds, one match stands out. In the game against Essex on a less-said-the-better wicket at Leyton, Yorkshire scored no more than 104 and yet won by an innings and 33 runs. In the first innings Hirst took seven for 12 and, in the second, five for 17. Even sober *Wisden* released a superlative more than once, and actually described Hirst's bowling as 'terrific', a word not lightly bandied about in 1901. When, half a century later, I reminded Hirst of these triumphs, he pulled a face.

'Ah,' he said, 'you should have seen my figures in that Somerset match—one for 189!'

The Somerset match. This was one of cricket's historic games, a game nearer to popular fiction than prosaic fact, in which Somerset, after being dismissed for a song in their first innings, piled up a gargantuan score in their second— this was when Hirst took one for 189—and eventually obliterated Yorkshire's second effort as with an ink-eraser, winning the match by 279 runs. When the last Yorkshire wicket fell, Sammy Woods, usually a loquacious character, did not speak, but rushed out of the Headingley ground, leaped into a cab, set off furiously toward the hotel where his team were staying, rushed into the bar and finally broke silence with the one resplendent word: 'Champagne!'

The period, you remember, was that of the Boer War, and many a cricketer was soldiering on the South African veldt. F. S. Jackson, the greatest Yorkshire all-rounder after Hirst and Rhodes, was an officer in the Yorkshire Yeomanry, and it happened that one evening he was inspecting his lines. The barbed wire suddenly twitched and from under its lowest strand crawled a scrubby, unshaven figure in ragged khaki, who was plainly either a scarecrow or an escaped prisoner of war. Inside the wire the scarecrow scrambled upright and saluted.

'Colonel Jackson, sir?'

'That's so.'

'Then, excuse me, sir.' The scarecrow's voice, speaking in the rich tones of the West Riding, expressed the grave concern demanded by a serious military situation. 'How did Yorkshire get on again' Somerset?'

'It was a bad do. Yorkshire lost by 279 runs.'

'Well, by gow ——'

'Here, where are you off to?'

'I'm off back to t'Boers!'

II

The year 1902 saw one of cricket's most dramatic seasons: Yorkshire won the county championship with the loss of one match, Somerset being once more at their giant-killing game; the Australians toured triumphantly, exhibiting the glory of Trumper between showers; England lost a tremendous rubber by three runs; and George Hirst was twice involved in the fantastic dismissal of the otherwise all-conquering visitors for less than 40 runs. It was not quite one of his overmastering seasons, yet it contained three or four of the heroic deeds by which to this day he is in our flowing cups freshly remembered. These will be described in their due place. His bowling feats in county cricket were not spectacular, though of genuine value at need. Often he was put on to bowl early, sent down a few overs, mainly maidens, and then gave place to either Rhodes or Haigh. In those magical years, two out of Yorkshire's three famous bowlers were *always* on top of the world. Sometimes it was Rhodes and Hirst; sometimes it was Rhodes and Haigh; in 1903 all three were very close together and were all successful. In 1902 Haigh and Rhodes were the leading bowlers in the country with 158 for just under 13 runs each and 213 for just over. By comparison Hirst's 83 for 20 apiece looked a modest bag, but he made his mark as a Test cricketer.

He had done little in Australia in 1897-8 and nothing in England in 1899, but in the first Test of 1902, played at

Birmingham on 29th, 30th, and 31st May, he had his place, and proved himself worthy of it, in what shrewd (if older) judges have reckoned the greatest England eleven in history. England, winning the toss, batted on a plumb wicket and lost the masters, Fry, MacLaren, and Ranjitsinhji, for 35; then F. S. Jackson joined Tyldesley and the game was slowly but firmly pulled round. Jackson left at 101 and Lilley went two runs later. England were in jeopardy again. Then came Hirst, and from the first he played one of his stubborn, back-to-the-wall, all-right-get-me-out-if-you-can, characteristically Yorkshire innings. With Tyldesley he put on almost 100 in just over an hour and England by the end of the day were on their way to a big score. It rained heavily during the night, and the knowing ones thought that when play was resumed on a wet pitch the following afternoon England's captain would declare at once. MacLaren shrewdly decided, however, that his bowlers should not be asked to start their attack with a wet and slippery ball, and so let his two batsmen go on with their unfinished partnership for another 25 runs. When he declared, Rhodes had scored 38 not out. Not a bad effort for a No. 11.

Then followed the most fantastic Test innings between Spofforth's match of 1882 and Laker's of 1956. Within an hour Australia were all out for 36, of which Trumper had courageously made half. The light was poor, but no one has ever seriously claimed that the wicket was exceptionally bad. The bowling figures were:

	Overs	Mdns	Runs	Wkts
Hirst	11	4	15	3
Rhodes	11	3	17	7
Braund	1	0	1	0

Figures normally speak for themselves, but concerning these C. B. Fry expressed an unorthodox opinion: 'Well as Rhodes bowled, it was Hirst who was responsible for the débâcle. This is the best instance I know of the bowler at the other end getting wickets for his colleague.'

(During my visit to Kirkheaton I recalled this historic feat. 'That's nowt,' said First Crony. 'The two of 'em came up here and put Slaithwaite out for 9. George Herbert took five for 2 and Wilfred took five for 3.' 'That's right,' added Second Crony, 'there were four byes, because our stumper was frightened of George Herbert.')

In the Birmingham innings there were three wides, but I have never been able to find who bowled them, though I am fairly certain it was not Rhodes. His, of course, was the more dazzling performance, but the two attacked as a single double-edged weapon and were backed by splendid fielding. Behind the stumps Lilley was as quick as a pickpocket and Braund took one catch by an anticipatory leap from slip to what we now call leg-slip at which old men marvel to this day. A shocked Australia followed on and scored 8 for none; then it rained for twelve hours and it was impossible to start again till after tea on the third (and last) day. Australia made 46 for two and that was that. England had undoubtedly been robbed of victory by the weather.

On the Sunday the Australians travelled to Leeds. It was hardly within the bounds of possibility that the next day these unhappy warriors should be locked in a struggle even deadlier than the Test match from which they had escaped. What England could not do, Yorkshire did. It was a battle of giants indeed. The pitch was treacherous to the point of high treason and the Australians, batting first, fought an uphill fight from the fall of the first wicket. Victor Trumper, the most masterly batsman on evil pitches in cricket history, gave one of the most resplendent performances of a career lit with splendour. He was top scorer with 38 and none of his many centuries was finer. When he went, caught by Denton from a heaven-kissing skier, the side collapsed before Hirst and Jackson, and but for a buccaneering duet by Nos. 9 and 10, Australia would never have reached a total of 131. Yorkshire, fighting gamely, fared rather worse. Denton and T. L. Taylor reached the twenties and Hirst and Rhodes battled their way toward 12 each as if these scores of a dozen represented the supreme effort of their lives. To be only 24 behind on the first innings was a brave achievement in itself.

What followed was plainly impossible. It merely *happened*. Jackson bowled right-hand medium-fast and dead straight; Hirst was swift and his swerve was deadlier. The Australians' start was only moderately bad; they had reached 20 for three when Hirst bowled the almost unbowlable Trumper with a ball of a lethal quality hardly seen again until Alec Bedser bowled Bradman with such another in 1948. It was, Hirst believed, the best ball he ever bowled in his life. Then, with only three runs added, the whole side were out. It was as though a candle had been extinguished. Hirst bowled Noble and Armstrong, and then Jackson finished off the rest of them, three wickets in five balls, as though sweeping them up into a dustpan. The figures were:

	Overs	Mdns	Runs	Wkts
Hirst	7	4	9	5
Jackson	7	1	12	5

But wait. Yorkshire needed only 48 to win and had the fight (and fright) of their lives in getting them. Taylor was top scorer with 11 and never were 11 runs bought with greater expenditure of toil and sweat. It was Irving Washington (9 not out) who made the winning hit, while Hirst, hanging on grimly at the other end, made none not out.

It was a drenching summer, comparable with the hideous season of 1958, and the second Test, at Lord's, lasted less than two hours. The rest of it was drowned, full fathom five, in rain. The third Test, played at Sheffield, spelled

England's downfall, a game in which the Australians played finely and every possible misfortune, short of an earthquake, fell on the stricken Englishmen. Ranjitsinhji was suffering from a badly strained leg and could not play; Barnes, chosen at the last moment in place of Lockwood, bowled splendidly in the first innings, took six for 49, and then cracked up. Bad light descended on the first evening, and on the second morning play continued on a beastly pitch which, almost as though in spite against England, mildly improved as the Australian second innings began. Its highlight was a fiercely hostile innings by Hill, and only some deadly bowling by Rhodes kept the Australians' score within bounds. In the fourth innings of this grim game Jessop was sent in first with Abel and England left off on the second evening with their score at 73, three-quarters of which were contributed by Jessop, batting vigilantly but hitting very hard. In the morning the pitch was unspeakable and wickets tumbled abjectly before Noble and Trumble. Only Jackson stayed for an hour with the heroic MacLaren. The rest was ruin; the last five wickets fell for 33 runs, and England were one down in the series.

Hirst's contribution to the fourth Test at Manchester resembled that of the famous dog in the Sherlock Holmes story. The remarkable thing is that he did not play and this was the reason why, in the opinion of an enraged West Riding, England lost the match. He was one of the twelve originally selected, but on the morning of the match the captain gazed in irritation at the slow soft wicket, remembered that Fred Tate, the Sussex slow bowler, was a member of the twelve, and left out Hirst. I well remember—I was eight years old at the time—the convulsive shudder that passed through Yorkshire like a seismic tremor, when the news of this incredible folly spread. Jessop, too, had been omitted from the twelve, but it was the dropping of Hirst which was for us the unpardonable sin.

MacLaren, England's captain, lost the toss and returned to the dressing-room with the cheerful announcement: 'It's all right, boys, they're batting; the sun's coming out; we've only to keep 'em quiet till lunch, and then . . .' At lunch-time the score was 173 for one—repeat 173 for one—and Victor Trumper had made 104. That was Trumper's idea of being kept quiet till lunch. The gods, unjust as always, punished the hapless Tate for the sins of others. Under their malevolence he bowled ineffectively, missed a vital catch at a critical moment and when he went in at No. 11, with England wanting eight to win, he saw the rain come down in a true Manchester torrent and scuttled back to the pavilion. When at last he returned to the wicket under a watery sun, he snicked a four off the first ball he received and was bowled, hook, line and sinker, by the fourth. The match was lost by three runs as surely as if it had been by an innings and 300. Rhodes had bowled with the utmost steadiness in each innings and Jackson had hit a memorable century, but this was not enough. The cricketing public of Yorkshire were not appeased. If the ground at that moment had opened and swallowed captain and selection committee, as it had once swallowed Korah, Dathan and Abiram, all Yorkshire would have felt that justice was manifestly seen to be done.

But, even at this late hour, the gods relented. For the fifth Test at the Oval, sanity returned to the selectors. Jessop and Hirst, the two who should never have been left out, were brought back and in the most dramatic game in cricket history (which the same I am free to maintain) England won by one wicket. Even though the rubber was lost, victory in this game was glorious. The game will always, and rightly, be known as Jessop's match, because it enshrined one of the most glorious feats of courageous hitting ever achieved by mortal cricketer. Ajax defied the lightning, but Jessop brought lightning of his own. In the second degree it might

have been called Hirst's match, for as Wilfred Rhodes told
me half a century later: 'If George hadn't saved the follow-
on in the first innings—and it was a near do—nobody can
say what would have happened.' In the third degree it
might have been called the 'Get-'Em-In-Singles' match, with
immense credit to the two Yorkshiremen, Hirst and Rhodes.
This is a tale that old men tell in the chimney corner, and it
will be told again in its place. It is enough here to say that
Hirst's bowling, regaining the deadly swerve it was thought
to have lost, broke the back of Australia's first innings; and
that his scores of 43 and 58 not out were, apart from Jessop's,
the most valuable contributions to this famous victory.

III

Yorkshire did not win the championship in 1903 and had
to be content with third place. It was one of those seasons
when misfortune comes, not in single spies, but in battalions.
Irving Washington, hero of Yorkshire's victory over Australia, broke down in health, Tunnicliffe had his hand split
while batting, and early in the season Hirst damaged a calf-
muscle. This injury kept him out of the side for several
games. It was, roughly speaking, during this early period
that a weakened Yorkshire incurred most of their losses—
losses from which a brilliant recovery was not quite enough
to take them to the top. 'Beyond all doubt,' said *Wisden*,
'Hirst was the best all-round man of the year.' He succeeded
in bowling, as the season went on, with the baffling swerve
that he seemed temporarily to have mislaid the year before.
When he came back into the side after his damaged leg had
recovered, he found that he had lost some of his speed, but
had gained in cunning and deadliness.

His batting average of 47 was his highest so far and his
bowling average of just under 15 his lowest. These figures
were impressive, but they did not truly show his power and
gaiety with the bat and his happy hostility with the ball.

Not only did he top his county's batting and bowling, but in all England's batting figures he came third, with no one but the majestic masters, Fry and Ranjitsinhji, above him. Here you see him, swiftly moving into what we might, without exaggeration, call his 'great' period, and no all-rounder except Rhodes has ever stayed on the heights so long. For the next ten years Hirst never failed to do the double, and it was sustained achievement at this level which led Lord Hawke to call him 'the greatest county cricketer of all time'.

It was a season stuffed with doughty deeds. Before his breakdown at Old Trafford in the Roses match, he had already hit a jolly century against Worcester, and had twice taken six wickets for 34 runs, once against Essex and once against Gloucestershire. As soon as he was back in harness, he not only hit a lusty 120, but followed up his century with five for 32 and four for 44 against Kent. You can imagine that the men of the hop-county wondered if they would ever survive the onslaught of this terrible fellow. There was a 153 against Leicestershire, ended over-eagerly by a run-out, a 142, full of daring pulls, against Somerset, and a near-century against Notts. (Who in this unadventurous age gets stumped at 99?) Counted worthy of higher esteem in Yorkshire than any centuries were his 58 and 69 not out scored off Lancashire bowling in John Tunnicliffe's benefit match at Headingley. Hirst was one of nature's risers to the occasion and, formidable though he could be at almost any time, he was twice as formidable against the beloved enemy in a Roses match.

No longer were the headshakers declaring that he must concentrate either on his batting or his bowling. He had shown himself master of both. With all his prodigal output of high scores, he still retained the necessary vigour for some bowling feats as well; seven for 36 in the return game with Notts and six for 26 against Gloucestershire. In spite of such a performance, the Gloucestershire game, strictly

GEORGE HIRST IN HIS EARLY COUNTY DAYS

'He retained throughout life the spirit of that Kirkheaton lad;
sturdiness, good temper, and a determination to use bat, ball
and hands to the greatest advantage of his side.'

'The Creator's model for a Yorkshireman'

Ready to attack the bowler

Attacking the batsman

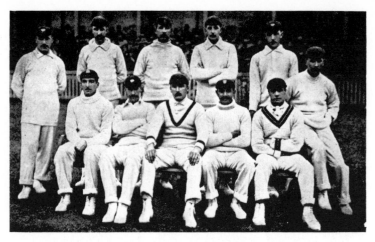

THE ENGLISH TEAM V. AUSTRALIA, EDGBASTON, 1902
Back row: G. H. Hirst, A. A. Lilley, W. H. Lockwood, L. C. Braund,
W. R. Rhodes, J. T. Tyldesley. *Front row:* C. B. Fry, F. S. Jackson,
A. C. MacLaren, K. S. Ranjitsinhji, G. L. Jessop.

*This is considered by many to be the best balanced of all
English teams*

YORKSHIRE CHAMPIONS, 1908
Hardisty, Bates, Newstead, Rothery, Myers, J. Hoyland (scorer)
Wilkinson, Haigh, Hirst, Lord Hawke, Hunter, Denton, Rhodes.

Lord Hawke's favourite side

speaking, was not Hirst's match, for in their second innings Rhodes and Haigh virtually exterminated their opponents for 36. An even madder match was the return game at Huddersfield against Worcestershire. The weather was vile: on the first day there was no play; on the second, it was restricted to an hour and three-quarters, and on the third to two hours. Yet in that exiguous time Yorkshire declared at 76 for one and came near to winning the match by an innings. Once more the astonishing fact emerges that although Hirst took five for 18 in Worcester's first innings total of 24, the insatiable Rhodes claimed five for 4.

Finally, in this dramatic year, the game with Surrey at the Oval was one on which Yorkshiremen in these bleaker days can only look back as a wistful and beautiful memory. Yorkshire made 254, a moderate total for a good batting side in those days, and still they won by an innings and nearly 100 runs. Yet it is the bowling figures which are most instructive and characteristic:

	First Innings				Second Innings			
---	Overs	Mdns	Runs	Wkts	Overs	Mdns	Runs	Wkts
Hirst	17.3	5	35	6	12.4	4	32	4
Rhodes	17	3	43	4	12	1	38	6

Such an attack called for no reinforcement. Hirst and Rhodes carried all before them and it was performances of this quality which won for the pair of them an invitation to tour Australia the following winter.

CHAPTER FIVE

Australian Summer and After

'In far Australia the English were sharpening their wickets.'
—Ernest Hemingway

I

IT WAS A poor side; at least, so the experts said. That is what the experts frequently say, as they undoubtedly said of Sir Leonard Hutton's victorious tourists in 1954-5. The 1903-4 side were captained by young P. F. Warner, who still remains young at eighty-four, and, though for one reason or another they lacked the talents and glamour of MacLaren, Fry, Jackson, Ranjitsinhji, and Jessop, they fought the good fight and brought home the Ashes, an achievement in which sides more distinguished-looking on paper have failed before and since.

There is a general belief that Hirst was a better player in county than in representative matches; certainly he was a superlative Yorkshireman, but his deeds in Tests and on tour, especially at vital moments, should not be 'damned with faint praise'. There is nothing in the averages to tell you which runs were scored off easy bowling on a plumb wicket and which were fought for one by one in a man's finest hour by toil and tears. If we could isolate Hirst's efforts in emergencies, his Test record would stand high.

He was by temperament a 'good tourist' and his unquenchable spirits and friendly good nature would have been an invaluable asset to any band of pilgrims. Nor were his actual achievements negligible. In the second State match against Victoria he made 92 and in the third, against New South Wales, he hit up 66, 'pulling like mad', as a Sydney

spectator said. In the first Test, he came in when the
England eleven, worn with the ardours and endurances of a
furious struggle and needing 194 to win on the sixth day, had
lost their first four wickets for 83. Any other man might have
been weighed down by anxiety. Not so George Hirst.
Taking one of his tremendous pulls at his first ball he was
almost caught at short leg by Laver. ('I hit it with all my
strength,' he told me long afterwards; 'I thought it had gone
right through Frank.') In company with the steadfast
Hayward, he put on over 100 runs and, when Hayward was
out, went on to carry out his bat for 60 as England completed their triumph.

He did little in the second Test at Melbourne—that match
belonged to Rhodes and Tyldesley, and to Trumper, too,
though he fought on the losing side. This was the game
played on Melbourne's notorious sticky wicket, of which
Hirst said wryly, 'When I was in Australia before, I nobbut
saw one wet wicket and that was hung up to dry!' But in
the third, one of the two games out of five that England lost,
Hirst fought a series of valiant rearguard actions, scoring 58
in the first innings and 44 in the second. The victorious
Australians agreed that, while Hirst was still in, no English
side was ever beaten. Until he was out, the fight went on.
When, bowling in the fifth Test in Melbourne's sticky heat,
he failed to find his length, he seized the ball every time a
wicket fell at the other end and bowled away till the next
man came in. He did not get the newcomer, but his spirit
was unquenchable. Scores in up-country matches naturally
did not count in the first-class averages, but Hirst thoroughly
enjoyed such jaunts into the back-blocks, giving the spectators immense value in entertainment. Many of the 'diggers'
drove long distances from remote stations to see his tremendous powers of hooking and pulling, and there is a record of
only one that was disappointed. In the first innings of the
game against Newcastle and District Hirst was out for four.

Retiring to the refreshment bar for the comfort of a glass of
beer he overheard a voice say: 'That Hirst, he's no flaming
good.' George Hirst was not revengeful, but that remark
had to be paid for. He therefore visited retribution, not
upon the speaker, but upon the batsmen, bowlers and
fielders of the Newcastle side. After taking five wickets for
30, he asked his captain as a favour to let him open the
second innings. He then hit up 50 in double-quick time and
with tremendous power, as if each hook for four or pull for
six was a hammer-stroke of righteous retaliation.

II

In the championship of 1904 Yorkshire finished second to
Lancashire, though not as close a second as they would have
wished. If Lancashire had not escaped (by great good
fortune) from defeat in Hirst's benefit match on August
Bank Holiday, the final reckoning might have been different.
Throughout the season Hirst rode, as he was to ride for
several years yet, on the top of his world. His was a nature,
robust, homely, zestful, that no success could spoil. This was
the year of his benefit, granted to him for 'twelve years of
splendid service', and he had still many years to come. A
cricketer's benefit normally marks his autumn; Hirst's
seemed only a day in his long high summer.

For the first time he scored 2,000 runs and took 100
wickets. No Yorkshireman had reached these heights before;
hitherto the feat seemed a monopoly of Gloucestershire men;
now Hirst was raising himself to the lordly ranks of Grace,
C. L. Townsend, and Jessop. And all this was achieved
under the pain and handicap of a strained leg, which he
declined to rest. In the game against Somerset, for instance,
he hit an aggressive 90 not out, limping heavily all the time.
This lameness interfered with his fierce bouncing run up to
the bowling crease and took the sharp edge off his pace, but
his accuracy was unimpaired and, though he did not secure

his hundredth wicket till late in August, he did many fine things with the ball, not least the devastating spell of six for 42, which he unleashed in his benefit match against Lancashire, after having rescued his own side from initial batting failure with a hard-hit 65. Whatever quantity of energy was needed, he could provide more. His reward in his benefit match was high and amounted to £3,703, of which I can only say that I would rather have what that sum could buy in 1904 than what four times as much can buy now.

Of his eight centuries, only two, with which he contributed to the higher education of Oxford and Cambridge, were levied on easy bowling. Apart from 152 against Hampshire, 108 against Surrey, and 140 against Essex, almost all his bigger scores were fought for under difficulties, his back to the wall. His 157 against Kent pulled a virtually hopeless game round into a creditable draw, after Yorkshire had been nearly 200 behind on the first innings and had lost two for none in their second. Against Middlesex his 103 formed the ladder by which Yorkshire climbed to safety from the depths.

III

An Australian side toured England once more in 1905 and were heavily defeated by an eleven captained by F. S. Jackson in the only two Test matches that were finished. Just for that season Jackson bestrode the cricket world like a colossus. This is not the place to describe how he headed, almost insolently, the Test averages in both batting and bowling and, to the Australian captain's accumulative exasperation, won the toss all five times. His personal triumph is relevant to the fact that Yorkshire won the county championship, despite his absence during all five Tests and that of Rhodes (four), Hirst (three), Haigh (two), and Denton (one).

Hirst's part in his county's success was again absolutely vital. Without him they would have been a body without a spinal column. The strain that had affected his damaged leg was by no means wholly cured and this meant that he always bowled under difficulties and in a good deal of pain. Yet such was his bodily strength and the pluck which supported it that he once more took his 100 wickets, and his batting was as rich and powerful as ever. Because of doubts about his unsound leg he was not picked for the first and second Tests, but in the third he batted well for 35 and 42 not out; in the fourth he scored 25 but did little bowling, for it was Brearley and Rhodes who shouldered that particular task.

In county games Hirst took seven for 48 against Somerset, and twice had five for 43, once against Kent and once against Surrey. His ordinary batting feats—he made five hundreds in all—were dwarfed by two gigantic ones. High in all the records stands his 341 against Leicestershire, the biggest score ever made by a Yorkshireman until Hutton's famous 364 against Australia at the Oval thirty-three years later. Leicestershire, who had started off on a shirt-front wicket, amassed a total of 419. When Hirst went in, Yorkshire were 22 for three wickets; when he was out, so to speak, three centuries later, they had reached 515. He was at the crease for seven hours and this was half an hour less than Trevor Bailey took to make 61 at Brisbane in 1958. While Hirst made 341, only two other men made more than 20. In this mammoth effort he hit a six and 53 fours, which is rather a large number for a man playing under strong restraint. The scorers must have been almost as tired as he was. And Yorkshire had almost left themselves time to get Leicester out at the second attempt. It is such matches as these which suggest that the older cricketers sometimes got through more work in three days than is customary in the present era.

His other enormous score was 232 not out, made against Surrey at the Oval. As in the game with Leicester, he played very nearly a lone hand; only one of his partners scored over 40 and only two others made double figures. In the same game he took five wickets for 43 runs. No doubt he had some affection for Surrey; they brought out the best in him almost as regularly as Lancashire did. In the return game at Headingley, scores were tiny and Yorkshire were set only 32 to win. So positively murderous, however, was the bowling of N. A. Knox, the fastest bowler between Kortright and Larwood, that five wickets fell in the rugged battle to get them. But not George Hirst's. On that day and against that bowling his 9 not out was an exploit of the utmost fortitude. The season's final deed of noble note was his 90 against Essex. Yorkshire had followed on 423 behind and then lost their first wicket without a run. This left them the task of remaining alive for a whole day against exceedingly hostile bowling. The task was accomplished. Hirst remained unbeaten until almost the end for his 90, and Ernest Smith, a natural-born hitter, played a mortal hour for nought not out. The struggle was homeric but the day was saved. Smith afterwards described that innings as his martyrdom.

CHAPTER SIX

'You're Twice as Happy . . .'

*'When you're both a batter and a bowler, you're twice as happy;
you enjoy yourself twice as much.'*—George Herbert Hirst

I

THE GREATEST of his great years was now approaching,
a year whose achievements recall the slightly incredible
exploits of W. G. Grace in 1876. The year 1906 was not all
honey for Yorkshire; this was the season in which they lost
the championship by one run. It was their defeat by
Gloucestershire in their last game by that 'narrowest of
margins' that allowed Kent to slip past them to the top.
Nevertheless, it was a splendid year for individual Yorkshiremen: batsmen like Denton and Tunnicliffe and bowlers like
Rhodes and Haigh excelled in their own especial arts, while
to George Hirst 1906 brought triumphs untouched by mortal
cricketer, before or since. To score 2,000 runs in a season is
the privilege of a specialist batsman; to take 200 wickets is
the comparatively rare achievement of a specialist bowler,
usually of a slow, easy-actioned, energy-preserving type.
That one man, a naturally powerful, forcing batsman and a
fast bowler with a bounding run and a full swinging arm,
who put every ounce of strength into each delivery, should
perform a kind of double 'double', was a miracle of dynamic
vigour, both in body and spirit. It was the triumph of a man
in the prime of manhood and will-power, of a man whose
chief quality was sheer wholeheartedness. There is nothing
in any other sport to compare with it; in cricket, there had
been nothing like it since W.G.'s storming days of the 1870s.
When asked if he thought any other cricketer would repeat

54

the marvel, Hirst replied thoughtfully: 'I don't know, but whoever does will be very tired.'

II

By 28th June he had taken his hundredth wicket and he went on from there with unflagging zest until September. His best individual match, which was characteristic of the whole season, was the last of the county games, played against Somerset at Bath, where he made 111 and 117 not out and took six wickets for 70 and five for 45. It is not an especially rare feat to make two centuries in a match, but I do not know of any cricketer who ever captured eleven wickets as well. Even his giant strength was becoming taxed by this time and he could feel that virtue had gone out of him. He confessed, at least, that after the third day he could do with a good night's sleep.

Figures, it is said, prove little; Hirst's 1906 figures, on the contrary, prove much. Yet even these, in their sheer impressiveness, do not tell more than one side of the story; they do not show how, when runs were badly needed on an abominable wicket, Hirst would almost always make them, or how, when the enemy seemed to be coasting easily home, he would suddenly break the back of their batting with a lethal spell.

On top of all this, when not batting and bowling, he was the best mid-off in the world at a time when the off-drive, virtually jet-propelled, was the favourite stroke of the world's most elegant batsmen. Men like Palairet, Spooner, and R. E. Foster revelled in the off-drive but they could not get many past George Hirst. The only cricketer I have ever seen who could compare with the Hirst of 1906 for sheer enjoyment of batting, bowling, *and* fielding was Learie Constantine.

All through the season Hirst was in the forefront of the battle, and his six centuries were not made on what the hymn calls 'flowery beds of ease'. His first 100 against Kent on a difficult wicket at Catford, was combined with a deadly spell of bowling, seven for 33; his second was combatively built up under heavy fire against Warwickshire at Edgbaston, with only one other man in the side making over 20. His best scores, as often happens, were not centuries at all. His 58 in the low-scoring Roses match on Whit Monday showed the boldest batting on his side, who were, to put it mildly, a little over-awed by the pace of Walter Brearley. When it was Lancashire's turn to bat, Hirst's bowling (six for 20) left the Lancashire batsmen in a complete daze, beaten by its pace and bamboozled by its swerve.

In the return game Lancashire looked at first like sweeping to their revenge, but after they had driven Yorkshire into a corner, so that with half their second innings wickets down they were still only 66 ahead, Hirst stepped once more into the breach and stayed there, steadfast, immovable, until his county had attained a winning lead. He seemed always to be there, and in his element, at 'the pinch of the game'.

In the second match against Kent he pulled the game right round with a gallant 93 in the second innings, and his 89 not out against Derbyshire at Sheffield turned a doubtful issue into victory. Not that his supreme efforts were crowned with success every time: the 87 that he made against Surrey at the Oval almost, but not quite, snatched the game from the fire, whilst against Notts at Dewsbury he nearly bowled his heart out to take fourteen wickets in the match for 97, but this was not enough. Over his dead body, you might almost say, Notts won by 25 runs. At Headingley he took seven for 18 and five for 48 in a runaway victory against Leicestershire, whose first innings reached only 34, and on a fast wicket at Hull he captured five for 15 in Worcestershire's total of 25. (Admittedly, a young bowler named Sedgwick took the other five wickets for 8, but this, sadly enough, is almost his only claim to remembrance.) On Hirst went, right to the end, and, tired or not, in the final match of the season, Champion County *v.* the Rest of England, he batted and bowled as though the fun and the fighting of a glorious year lay before and not behind him.

III

He had, as we have seen, taken his 100 wickets early in the season. His two hundredth was for his devotees a matter of hope and speculation. Would he capture it before the end of the season? He had not done so when the Scarborough Festival began in September. When I recently visited Kirkheaton, I called on Hirst's younger sister, a charming lady, who lives in a trim little house with a garden that was then ablaze with marigolds. She showed me the ball, silver-mounted, with which he took his last two wickets in the first-class game and she told me the story of his two-hundreth wicket in 1906.

Among the thousands of spectators who went to the Festival game for the pleasure of seeing Hirst get his two-hundredth wicket were two elderly ladies who had a vested interest in the matter. One was his mother; the other was Wilfred Rhodes's mother. The desired result was slow in coming. Hirst bowled wholeheartedly, as he always did, but the batsmen defended with obstinacy and some good fortune, and when a wicket fell, it fell perversely at the other end. The tension mounted. At last the strain grew so great that neither of the ladies could bear it a moment longer. There was only one thing to do and that was to get as far away as possible from this intolerable stress of waiting. Quietly they slipped from their seats and made their way slowly through the massed crowds toward an exit. They were a little breathless as they walked slowly down the North Marine Road. Suddenly from behind them a roar of cheering broke, swelled, and went rolling up into the sky. George Herbert had taken his two-hundredth wicket.

And they had missed the sight of it.

CHAPTER SEVEN

Still on the Heights

'His off-drives, mellow as brown ale, and crisp
Merry late cuts, and brave Chaucerian pulls . . .'
—William Kerr

I

WHEN THE height of achievement has been reached, it is
not within nature to avoid some period of decline, and 1907
was for Hirst something of a mild anti-climax. The season
was a wretchedly wet one and Yorkshire lost more full days
from rain than they had ever lost before or were to lose
until the lamentable season of 1958. Two home matches
were abandoned without a ball being bowled; many lost a
whole day or a day and a half, and scarcely one game in
Yorkshire's county programme saw three full days' cricket.
These conditions cast a dark cloud over high-scoring
batsmen and fast bowlers; Hirst did not make his 2,000 runs,
nor indeed take his 200 wickets, though, to do him justice,
only one bowler in England took more wickets and only four
had a better average.

He had no great success in his three Tests against the
touring South Africans, though he took five for 54 against
them in a county game. In 1907 he did not make a single
century, a failure to be repeated in only one season between
then and his retirement. His next summer without a century,
in fact, was 1920. Even if there were no hundreds, there was
no dearth of substantial scores, and these regularly played
their part in his side's salvation. His 78 against Essex at
Leyton turned, with some help from Lord Hawke, a probable

defeat into victory, and twice his stubbornly courageous
batting—49 not out and 68 not out against Surrey at the
Oval, and 91 not out, his highest score, against Kent at
Canterbury—enabled Yorkshire to shake themselves free
from a desperate situation. Hirst was not, of course, the only
player to share in these recoveries, but he was usually their
inspiration. Sometimes it was Hirst and Denton; sometimes
Hirst and Tunnicliffe; sometimes Hirst and Rhodes; it was
almost monotonously Hirst and somebody.

Though he seldom had any chance of bowling on wickets
that were friendly to his tearaway style, he performed some
prodigious feats with the ball. He would probably have
regarded his six wickets for 26 against Cambridge University
and his five for 34 and five for 43 against Somerset as small
beer, but no one could think lightly of his fifteen wickets for
63 runs against Leicestershire. In this memorable game he
almost succeeded in polishing off the opposing batsmen in
one day. Admittedly the state of the pitch was hideous, but
Leicestershire were cast forth for 60 (Hirst, eight for 25);
Yorkshire, with a total of 114, did not do so much better;
and by the end of the day Hirst had captured the first four
wickets of Leicestershire's second innings at a cost of 11 runs.
This included a hat-trick, the victims being C. B. J. Wood,
King, and Knight, indubitably their county's best batsmen,
all of whom in their time had made their hundreds against
Yorkshire bowling. The following morning the tail-enders
shut their eyes, so to speak, and swung their bats and 27
more runs were hit off Hirst's bowling. In spite of this, it took
only half an hour to get rid of them and Hirst's final second
innings figures were seven for 38, which brought his final
match figures to fifteen for 63.

The game against Derbyshire on a similarly treacherous
pitch at Glossop showed another of those slightly terrifying
analyses which had a habit of studding the score-book at the
time:

	First Innings				Second Innings			
	Overs	Mdns	Runs	Wkts	Overs	Mdns	Runs	Wkts
Hirst	10.1	1	22	4	15	4	22	7
Rhodes	10	1	22	6	14.3	0	49	2

The exploit which Hirst himself esteemed most highly took place at Bramall Lane in the teeth of a powerful Middlesex eleven. In the visitors' second innings, while Rhodes's faultless length pinned the batsmen down, like moths on a card, Hirst at the other end appeared to whistle up exactly the kind of wind which would intensify—nay, almost ignite —his natural swerve. In the end his record read: nine for 45. In the score-book these figures looked all the more diabolical because seven out of the nine batsmen were clean bowled.

II

While neither he nor anyone else was ever likely to equal the marvels of 1906, Hirst had another stupendous year in 1908. His batting, as it had always been, was hard and strong, especially at need and against the most powerful opponents. His bowling, which started off with the slightly incredible match figures of twelve for 19 against Northamptonshire, placed him second among the year's bowlers; only Haigh had a better average and only Blythe took more wickets. Haigh's success was another proof that Yorkshire were doing finely.

Hirst's more substantial scores, 58 and 128 not out against Derby, 89 against Leicester and 96 against Middlesex, were nearly always obtained by fierce hitting on the leg-side, and at a stage where personal failure might have meant defeat for his side. Sometimes he would, for full measure, give his side the benefit of a double performance, as when he hit 74 and took five for 69 against Essex or when he scored a particularly defiant 50 (coupled with six wickets for 54) against Middlesex.

More often, however, it was one of his havoc-dealing spells
of bowling which turned a doubtful issue into a Yorkshire
victory. Such was the fury of his attack in the second
innings of the Surrey game at Headingley that once more
five of his six victims were clean bowled. (He and Haigh
between them clean bowled eight, one was caught at the
wicket, and the other was run out by a quick return from
Hirst at mid-off.) Even more vital to the result of the game
was his onslaught in the Roses match at Bramall Lane,
where with unimpaired energy he bowled forty-five overs
and took eleven wickets for exactly 8 runs each. And in the
home game with Notts he bowled at one end from start to
finish of the match and once more took eleven wickets at a
cost of slightly less than 8 runs apiece. No wonder Lord
Hawke looked on 1908 as very nearly Yorkshire's greatest year.

III

The summer of 1909 was one of incorrigibly evil weather for
England, Yorkshire, and George Hirst. England surrendered
the rubber to a by no means invincible Australian touring
side, losing two of three Tests that the rain permitted to
finish. Defeat, many people felt, was due less to the in-
feriority of England's players than to the eccentricity of
England selectors. Hirst played in four of the five matches—
only MacLaren and Lilley played in five—but, apart from
two excellent bowling performances, four for 28 and five for
58, in the only game that England won, he did not show
himself in his best fighting form. In that game he appeared
almost to hypnotize the Australians with his swerve, and his
energy never for an instant slackened. After that game his
Test record for the season was frankly poor.

He may have suffered from the cumulative tiredness of
so many hard seasons and certainly his untrustworthy leg
was subject to continuous heavy strain, but friends and
admirers were disappointed to note a temporary halt in the

lusty old vigour of his batting. After a hard-hit 80 against Derbyshire and a truly rumbustious 140 against Northants, his doings with the bat were but moderate. He seemed to be hoarding up his energies to inspire his bowling in the matches that really mattered. Even if, in a period of aberration, he had forgotten how to bowl, all his true skill, zest, and power would have returned to him for a Roses match. On a dark, damp day at Old Trafford, when Yorkshire had set the enemy no more than a quite modest total to win, he unleashed such a fury of swerve, verve, and velocity upon them that five wickets went rattling down for 6 runs. A. H. Hornby, Lancashire's captain, a man by no means lacking in courage, lunged out with one or two hostile hits, but soon after lunch the struggle ended. Yorkshire had won by 65 runs, and Hirst's figures, despite a little late rough handling from devil-may-care tail-enders, were no worse than six for 23.

There was the same gusto in his six for 20 against Surrey, obtained by bowling which swerved menacingly and got up awkwardly, and in his seven for 95 in Yorkshire's struggle with Middlesex at Headingley. In this game he made the ball leap to (and from) the bat's edge time after time, and old David Hunter, then in his twenty-first season, cannily accepted six catches behind the wicket in the one innings. It was, unhappily for Yorkshire, not quite the same with his six for 27 against Surrey in the return game at the Oval, for though Hirst's attack on a fiendish wicket was deadly, that of Rushby and Razor Smith was deadlier still and Yorkshire in their second innings were all out for 26, the humblest score in their strange eventful history. But that is another story.

IV

By the end of 1909 Hirst was thirty-eight years old and had been Yorkshire's prop and mainstay for seventeen full seasons. This, if you like, was a full cricketing life for even the sturdiest of men. The *Wisden* of 1910 devoted a number of pages to a detailed tabular record of his doings in first-class cricket. With a statistical ingenuity worthy of a better cause they showed how many runs he had made in the course of a full life for Under 30 *v.* Over 30 and how many wickets over a period of years he had taken against Liverpool and District; they also showed, perhaps more valuably, how he had up to the end of 1909 scored 26,050 runs, including 44 hundreds, taken 2,121 wickets, and headed his county's batting averages for six years in succession. The record did not actually say so, but there was about it all a kindly, valedictory touch which suggested that this good and faithful servant must now surely be leaning back, lighting his pipe and thinking, perhaps a little thankfully, of the peaceful pleasures of retirement.

Nothing, in 1910, was farther from George Hirst's thoughts. That year was one of his richest and best. More than ever he excelled in his own characteristic way, mainly as the deliverer of his side from desperate straits. Not even the coxswain of the Cromer lifeboat has effected so many daring rescues. Hirst was not always successful in averting defeat, but he loved to show the qualities of the good soldier: 'In war, resolution; in defeat, defiance.' An almost unlimited amount of defiance was demanded, for Yorkshire were experiencing the unhappiest season of Hirst's career. In the seventeen seasons between their first championship in 1893 and the beginning of that doleful summer they had won the chief honour eight times and never been lower down the ladder than its third downward rung. In 1910 they were eighth. Since the second World War Yorkshire players, if not Yorkshire spectators, have become inured to misfortunes, but in 1910 a fall to eighth place seemed like Lucifer's. My Step-Uncle Walter (if I may quote, just once, my amiably eccentric relative) said that the only match Yorkshire really enjoyed that summer was the fixture abandoned because of King Edward VII's funeral. This, however, was but the angry growl of a disillusioned patriot. The fact was, then as now, that Yorkshire folk take it ill to find themselves sampling life among the lowly. What to them seemed dire disgrace might, for other counties 'not so blest as they', have been a reasonably satisfactory position.

Whatever the county's woes, George Hirst was not to blame for them. But for his fighting efforts, Yorkshire's troubles might have been worse. Those critics who, the season before, had been wishing him a long and happy retirement, now sat up in gratified surprise to note that, as in his great days, he once more stood at the head of both Yorkshire's batting and bowling and that, according to the England tables, only Razor Smith and Colin Blythe could claim more wickets. He suffered something which, though less certain than death and taxes, comes to nearly all true cricketers soon or late: the experience of 'getting a pair'. This happened at Northampton and the county authorities are lax if they have not hung up, framed, in their pavilion, a copy of the card of the match, with these details underlined:

G. H. Hirst   b. Smith   o   b. Wells   o.

He gave some fine exhibitions of batting, scattering them broadcast over the programme: a resolute 90 against Hampshire at Bradford; a creditably Jessop-like 158 against Cambridge University; 103 and 88 against Warwickshire on the familiar home ground of Huddersfield; and, best of all, his match-winning 137 which enabled Yorkshire to beat Middlesex by two wickets. I saw the finish of this game on my first visit to Lord's. It was indeed my first visit to London, as a lad of sixteen, and the glory of it has remained with me to this day: the tremendous hitting of Denton and Hirst; the authentic breathless hush before the last over was bowled, and the generous acclamation of the London crowd, who knew great cricket when they saw it. It showed me, too, that George Hirst captured the imagination and affection of the crowd wherever he went.

Sometimes there were battles of sheer resistance, as against Sussex on a tricky wicket at Hull, and against Leicestershire at Headingley where his 66 represented half his side's score and saved the follow-on, though it could not save the game. If ever the wind conspired to abet his swerve, he could still tear through an opposition as if it were a paper hoop. This he did at Headingley where Worcester, set 160 to win, crumpled up in a struggle to reach 50. Hirst's share of the loot was seven wickets for 28 runs. When Derbyshire were dismissed for 75 at Bradford he and Booth bowled unchanged (Hirst five for 35, Booth five for 34); he also took six for 34 at Taunton against the ancient stubborn enemy, Somerset. Haigh disposed of the rest of the wickets and every man-jack but one of the lot of them was clean bowled.

But Yorkshire's feat of the season, which was in fact cricket's feat of the season, was performed, as were so many of Hirst's doughtiest deeds, in the second innings of a Roses match. Lancashire, who, after all, were the team of Tyldesley and MacLaren, made 229 on the first day—anyone may say that they should have scored more, but they were made to fight for each run. It was then their turn to set about the Yorkshire batsmen, and, with Brearley bowling like a demon, it was left to the tail-enders, Haigh and the new captain, E. J. Radcliffe, to salvage whatever could be recovered from the wreckage. Excited fieldsmen dropped a catch or two in sheer nervous tension; if they had not, the score would have been much smaller. As it was, when Lancashire went in again they were 77 ahead and had established, one would have imagined, a commanding lead. Once more it can be shown that nothing is more eloquent than a score-sheet:

A. H. Hornby b Hirst	6
A. Hartley c Newstead b Hirst	1
J. T. Tyldesley b Hirst	4
J. Sharp b Hirst	0
E. L. Wright b Hirst	4
A. C. MacLaren b Haigh	19
J. S. Heap not out	9
W. Huddleston b Hirst	3
H. Dean b Hirst	0
W. Brearley b Hirst	0
W. Worsley b Hirst	6
extras	9
	—
	61

Nine men, as you can see, had their stumps struck down;
Hirst's figures were nine for 23 and Haigh's one for 10.
When the Yorkshire club presented Hirst with the ball,
beautifully mounted, Schofield Haigh, that inveterate joker,
frowned portentously.

'Nay, George,' he said, 'it's half for me and half for thee;
we got the wickets.'

v

The summer of 1911 was fine and dry and smiled on England's cricket, but not on Yorkshire's. The county rose from
the eighth position in the championship to the seventh, a
definite but unflattering improvement. Glancing through
the scores, you will gain the impression that, with two outstanding exceptions, all Hirst's more spectacular deeds were
accomplished with the ball. Starting off with the capture of
six wickets for 26 against Derbyshire at Bramall Lane, he
secured match figures of ten for 105 against Worcestershire
and ten for 107 against Notts, not to mention a five for 54
against Hampshire and a six for 34 against Sussex.

In the return game against Sussex at Hastings, whither a shattered Yorkshire had retreated after two humiliating lickings from Hampshire and Kent, it seemed as if the northerners had screwed their courage to the sticking-point and muttered: 'Thus far and no farther.' In pursuit of this policy, they piled up a total of 522 for seven wickets and then won by an innings. Hirst's individual share of the huge total was 218, the third highest score of his career, and he belted the bowling right, left, and centre, as if demanding compensation for Yorkshire's lowly status and the chain of disasters with which the season seemed to be ending. He had twice stood as the main bastion against heavy defeat, with 75 against Middlesex and 87 against Surrey. But even so brilliant a piece of bowling as his five for 26 against Warwickshire at Harrogate failed to bring his county salvation, for in their second innings Yorkshire collapsed abjectly before those two formidable Franks, Foster and Field, whose bowling formed the spearhead of the attack which that year carried Warwickshire for the first time to the head of the table. If, while mauling the Sussex bowling at Hastings, George Hirst thought of those things, it helped to put an extra propulsive force into every one of his 34 fours.

Yet there were two matches that he might have rated of higher quality even than the one that gave him his highest score. One was the game at Worcester, in which he took nine first-innings wickets for 41 and then put on his pads to score a quick 100. The other was—I had nearly said, of course—the Roses match at Old Trafford, the sort of toe-to-toe struggle in which he revelled. His strength in such games was as the strength of ten, not so much because his heart was pure (and it was purer than the hearts of most sinful mortals), but because here was the beloved enemy, here was the foeman worthy of a Yorkshire warrior's steel. He made only 15 in the first innings but, when Lancashire took their turn, he bowled with far more than an ordinary player's force and fire, and in two spells sent down 35.4 overs, bowling the first man and the last, and taking four more wickets in between. The wicket was iron-hard and, when Yorkshire went in again, Brearley's deliveries kicked like wild mules from the pampas. Yet first Drake and then Hirst played him as if he had no terrors. Hirst defended by attacking and batted as though each ball had to be consigned to eternal punishment. His 156 was scored in quick time, even for those quick-scoring days, and when Lancashire batted a second time they were dismissed with ease. It was an anti-climax to the fiercest but most satisfying match of the season.

VI

In this second half of this weather-beaten century we often feel that the summer we are enduring at any given moment must be worse than any other. It is salutary to take down the Good Book, i.e. John Wisden's *Cricketer's Almanack*, for any year of the first half and see how wet it could be then. I would trust the *Wisden* of the past more firmly than the meteorological wisdom of the present. Broadly, the fact is that one year in four, or at best one year in three, gave cricket a decent summer. The year 1912 was as deplorable in its weather as any we can think of. Rain interfered wantonly with the Triangular Tournament played between England, Australia, and South Africa and made a sorry mess of the county championship. Yorkshire returned to the top of the table, and deserved their high estate, but the number of draws, caused by bad weather, was appalling, and draws, as Sammy Woods observed, are no use to anybody except for bathing. Hirst was not picked to play for England that year, either against Australia or South Africa, but in Yorkshire's drawn game against the former at Bramall Lane, he was top-scorer with a hard-hit 62; he also played a punitive innings of 65 against the South Africans at Huddersfield. Rain spoiled both these matches, as it did so many more. What was a comparatively poor year by Hirst's high standards was not necessarily a poor year in itself. Many an honest county stalwart would have been delighted with a record of 1,133 runs and 118 wickets, especially if this had been his tenth double in a row. Remarkable or not, the only other players to achieve the season's double were Frank Woolley, then in the springtime of his glorious career, Frank Tarrant, the Middlesex Australian, Albert Relf, H. L. Simms, and J. H. King, Leicestershire's finest all-rounder before George Geary. At forty-one Hirst was still in the highest flight.

He started well with the bat in a series of rain-drowned matches, missed two or three games because of an injured knee, and then compiled his solitary century of the season against Worcestershire. He was missed at long-on before he had scored. This was a slice of luck that was larger than his usual portion, and he proceeded to show his gratitude for this indulgence by an innings of swiftness and power. In bowling he did nothing spectacular, but when Yorkshire gained a handsome victory at Southampton over Hampshire after facing a first innings total of over 400, he had a match analysis of ten for 138. He then finished off his double at Taunton by taking twelve Somerset wickets for 67. Not bad for a bad year.

VII

In the next season, the last completely untroubled summer before the 1914-18 war, the sun shone brightly. For a change, county matches went on, uninterrupted by rain, for the whole of three days at a time. The make-up of the Yorkshire side was changing, and some of the great names were dropping out. Lord Hawke, Tunnicliffe, and Hunter had gone, and Haigh was completing his last county season before going as coach to Winchester. Such losses, especially that of Haigh, were hard to bear and might have been permanently crippling to a county less rich in talent, but the new men who kept coming in were cricketers of the highest quality: Roy Kilner, a left-handed all-rounder in the true Yorkshire tradition, shortish, sturdy, merry-eyed, cap ever askew; Major Booth, dark, tall, and handsome, one of Pudsey's inexhaustible band of heroes, fast bowler and hard-hitting batsman; and Alonzo Drake, a left-handed character-comedian from Honley, Huddersfield, who topped the county bowling figures and, among serious bowlers, came close to Colin Blythe near the head of the national table. There were also two young batsmen of whom cricket would hear more: Percy Holmes, who was later to retain for Yorkshire batting much of the dash and sparkle with which Denton now graced it, and Edgar Oldroyd, an almost impregnable defender on the worst of wickets.

Playing alongside these bright youngsters were two other cricketers who both possessed the secret of eternal youth. There was Rhodes, at thirty-six, supremely gifted in everything he touched, going in first for England and bowling less frequently but, at need, still bowling with a precision that was scientific and relentless. And there was Hirst, at forty-two glowing with energy and enthusiasm, as ready to drink delight of battle with his peers as he had ever been over the last score of years.

Once more he headed the Yorkshire championship tables in batting and, though his bowling figures were an odd decimal point or two less excellent than Drake's and Booth's, he once more captured his 100 wickets and several times propelled his side toward victory by exploits with both bat and ball. Against Gloucestershire he hit 54, after Yorkshire had started in a semi-palsied manner; then he went on to take six wickets for 70. Later, in a low-scoring game against Somerset, he took four for 33 and made 58, the highest individual score of the match.

He made a number of eighties and nineties in addition to his three centuries. The boldest of these was undoubtedly the 102 not out he made against Kent, the season's champions to whom Yorkshire eventually ran second. Set over 300 to make in the fourth innings Yorkshire lost Rhodes, Wilson, Denton, and Drake for 41 runs. Then Hirst joined Roy Kilner in a situation which, by all the canons of caution, called for vigilant defence. Hirst, without hesitation, threw caution to the winds. Instead of defending, he attacked; as the light began to fade he began to hit harder and harder, and when the rain finally closed in, over 150 runs had been added without the loss of a wicket and the game, once poised on the brink of disaster, had been transformed into an honourable draw.

His highest total in 1913 was 166 not out against Sussex; when he went in, the board read 22 for three. His other 100 was exacted from Surrey at the Oval, and in this game, as in so many, he was the architect of victory. In the final Gentlemen *v.* Players game at Scarborough he took no wickets, but scored 51 and 49 in a struggle that was contested at full stretch till the last hour of the last day and was won and lost by six runs.

This season saw Hirst's fourteenth and last double. It was also the last summer to run its full course in the sunshine before the shadow of war fell across it. It is a simple fact that throughout the season he batted as aggressively as ever he did. That he headed the county's batting averages goes without saying. As for bowling, it was not so much that his powers were waning, as that Yorkshire had at least three other attacking bowlers. Whoever heard of a fiercely fast bowler at the age of forty-three? Yet there were spells when he slew them. . . . In the first game of the season he set about the Northamptonshire batsmen with such elemental force that in one stint after lunch on the second day he took six wickets for 19. There was also a five for 94 in a hard-fought game at Leicester and, what pleased him most, a four for 31 in the return Roses match at Old Trafford.

VIII

And now the curtain was going up on the last act of cricket's pre-war stage. Cricket would come again, as (we pray on our knees) it will always come again. But it would not be the same. Cricket might show a resemblance to other theatrical forms: tragedy or farce or a kind of competent, indeed highly sophisticated, commercial drama. But never again could it be the elegant and scintillating comedy of manners on which the curtain fell in 1914.

In that year Hirst did not escape his share of injuries which are a professional cricketer's occupational risk, and thereby missed many matches. For the first time since 1903 he failed to do the double and, after an early onslaught of six for 34, he was able to bowl only about half the overs and take a little less than half the wickets of a normal season. His batting, on the contrary, showed no loss of the heroic element that had always been its outstanding quality. When Yorkshire were in peril of an innings defeat from Hampshire, he stayed with Denton till well over 300 runs had been added and the threat had faded. But this was no splice-sitting session, no grim watchnight service. The defence, in the hands of those two happy warriors, became a fierce attack and Hirst's share was 146.

His other two centuries were made against the less rigorous bowling of Northants and Somerset, but they were scored rapidly and in the cavalier manner that delighted spectators everywhere. He enjoyed making centuries; he probably enjoyed even more the sort of battle fought at Bradford against the powerful Surrey eleven, when he scored 48 and 55 and almost saved Yorkshire from defeat by his fighting efforts. This was the celebrated match in which Jack Hobbs hit a century that was magnificent even for him and included five sixes, one of which, off Drake, hit the pavilion clock and knocked back the hour hand.

'Nay, Jack,' protested Alonzo, sorely-tried victim of the

outrage, 'tha should have knocked her on to half-past six and we'd have been rid of thee!'

Off the first delivery of the next over Hobbs's partner hit a single, and with the next Hirst clean bowled Hobbs with a ball good enough to beat the master. It was a noble innings nobly ended.

An honour that fell to Hirst in June was an invitation to play in the match at Lord's which celebrated cricket's hundred years' tenure of the present ground. The sides comprised the M.C.C. team recently home from touring South Africa and a powerful eleven representing the Rest of England. As it turned out, the Rest proved much too strong for the tourists, and Hirst, who was in grand batting form at the time, was extremely unlucky to be run out for only 15.

As July fell shuddering into August, cricket paused. Those cricketers who were Reservists or Territorials disappeared quietly into the Services. There was a move, led by a now classic letter to the Press from W.G. himself, to stop cricket at once, but a contrary argument prevailed and the championship ran its course amid the encircling gloom. The Army took over the Oval and Surrey finished their programme at Lord's. Scarborough Festival, symbol of north-country relaxation, was abandoned. No one was to enjoy its gaiety again for five grim years.

CHAPTER EIGHT

Summer Returns

'God! but it's England,' then they said,
'And there's a cricket field.'
— T. C. P. Wilson

I

THE LIFE of the nation is of infinitely more importance than the small pleasant corner of it that is called cricket. Soon the young men, butchers, bakers, and cricketers, too, had gone off to train with the various regiments that they had joined. On many a cricket ground units of Kitchener's army were drilling. A number of the older and more eminent players, for whom cricket was their only profession, obtained jobs in munitions or in other war work. Thus they were able to turn out on Saturday afternoons for the local clubs which, being situated in the bigger industrial areas, were often members of such famous leagues as those that play exciting Saturday cricket in Yorkshire, Lancashire, and the Midlands. There was nothing of the 'sheltered' element in this, least of all with George Hirst, who was nearly forty-four years old. On the contrary, as was recognized much more fully in the second World War, there was much good sense in encouraging a morale-building policy for the workers who were making guns, shells, and army clothing at home. There were none of the glorious Commonwealth matches such as in the second war shed a special splendour on Lord's in defiance of flying bombs. On the other hand, there were plenty of local League games graced by the presence of such cricketing giants as Hobbs, Woolley, Barnes, and Rhodes, and in cricket of this kind Hirst played an honourable part. A particular friend of mine was captain of a team in the Bradford League for which Hirst played in some games. My friend put in his pocket the two guineas that formed the visiting professional's usual fee and together they went out to bat. They had great fun with the bat, as Hirst had later with the ball, as well. When the game was won, my friend said: 'Thank you, George, and what about your fee?'

'Now look,' said Hirst, 'I know you're not a rich club. Make it ten bob and I'll call it quits, but'—he solemnly winked—'don't give me away!'

He must have been, as Learie Constantine was twenty years later, the ideal club professional: a fast bowler, a keen-eyed, quick-footed hitter and an impassable fielder, ready at any time on the field to take charge of the game and, off it, to encourage the young players and hand on the unique wisdom of his counsel—rich, homely, humorous, and supremely practical—to a new generation.

II

All bad things—it is a truth forgotten in a pessimistic age— must come to an end. For many thousands of young men, returning from the war, the brightest promise of the year 1919 was the prospect of cricket's coming to life again. War had cut down, as it always does, many of the fairest and the best. Men as valued as Colin Blythe, the brilliant K. L. Hutchings of Kent, and 'Tibby' Cotter, the Australian fast bowler, had been killed, the mighty W.G. and Victor Trumper had died in 1915, and many cricketers, of less exalted status but of equally valiant heart, would see green fields no more.

Yorkshire's own losses were severe. Major Booth had been killed, as Hedley Verity was later to be killed, leading his men in an attack, and Alonzo Drake had died, as George Macaulay was to die, of an illness contracted on active service. These two brilliant youngsters had been their county's brightest prospect and their loss seemed irreparable. Now younger men must be sought out again. The finds of the year were young Herbert Sutcliffe, the batsman who was to partner Hobbs in many an England first-wicket stand, and Abe Waddington, a fast left-hand bowler with a classically beautiful action. These two were remarkable cricketers, but while Yorkshire were still searching for more first-class recruits, heavy demands continued to be made on the old guard. The old guard included Hirst, Rhodes, and Denton, and the combined contribution of these three to Yorkshire's championship victory in 1919 was more than impressive.

Rhodes, after being England's leading bowler and then going in to bat first for England, now became, at thirty-eight, and as if with effortless ease, England's leading bowler again. It was almost as if, in that first post-war season, nobody else really remembered how to bowl. Denton, a gay youngster of forty-five, batted with the apparently careless brilliance of a dashing undergraduate; and the doings of Hirst were what we should now describe as 'out of this world'.

Here was a man approaching his forty-eighth birthday, who had played his first county season twenty-eight years before. It might well have been expected that he would have burnt himself out with the sheer prodigal expenditure of his flaming energy. He might have tottered into retirement; he might, in the sad manner of some fading stars, have 'lagged superfluous' on cricket's stage.

He was undoubtedly on the stage, but if we may retain the metaphor without flogging it, so far from lagging, he was playing to crowded houses. There was only one man before him so to defy the hand of time: that was W.G., the Doctor, the Old Man himself; and there was only one after: that was Wilfred Rhodes.

From the manner in which Hirst began the season, you would have thought he could hardly avoid reaching his thousand runs in the first month of summer. I happened to see Yorkshire's first match against the M.C.C. at Lord's, for I was just back from foreign service myself, and longing for the music of bat and ball. Music, indeed, but it was not the charming tinkle of a Debussy, but the majestic sweep of a Beethoven. Yorkshire, winning the toss, were shot out cheaply; the M.C.C. proceeded to pile up a score of close on 500, the backbone of which was a gaily characteristic effort from Hendren. This, with its vigorous driving, pulling and hooking, looked as if, even at this early hour, it might be the finest innings of the year. When Yorkshire went in again they were 368 behind and, just to darken the sky a little further, they lost two quick wickets. They should then have 'come quietly'. Instead, they proceeded to run riot as though bowlers had no object in life but to be hit for six. Holmes, who had come into the side just before the war, made a Denton-like 99; Roy Kilner, smiling broadly all the time, perhaps at the joke of having got out of the army, made 120, and Hirst, batting with the same fire and fury as he had displayed at least a dozen years before, reached a total of 180 not out. Hendren, so to speak, had slain his thousands, but Hirst his tens of thousands. His driving and pulling had the power of divine wrath, and he kept up the pressure until Yorkshire were able to declare and retire from the contest with a highly creditable draw.

After Lord's, he made 80 against Cambridge University; then he took 120 from Essex in a successful fight to avoid the follow-on; and after that, with an unhappy Roses match in between, he scored 120 against Warwickshire. All this within a fortnight. In Yorkshire's next game he scored 88, in one more pull-for-the-shore-sailor innings against the Australian Imperial Forces team, and this almost, but not quite, brought victory.

Naturally he did not keep up the pace of this triumphal progress; it was hardly within human power to do so. All the same, there were some fine fighting innings later in the season, including an aggressive 82 not out against Gloucestershire and 61 against Middlesex, after Yorkshire had fallen behind on the first innings. In the Gentlemen *v.* Players match at Lord's his 50 not out was completely characteristic, for he came in when four wickets had fallen for 17 and went on imperturbably to carry out his bat, without much assistance from anybody.

In the first-class batting tables of the season, several batsmen came out above him, including Hendren, Hobbs, and Philip Mead, but none of these fine players was within ten years of Hirst's age.

During the season Hirst accepted the post of coach at Eton and, when September and Festival time came along, the crowd at Scarborough was larger and more enthusiastic than ever, partly because it was the first Festival after the war and partly because many people believed they might never see George Hirst on a cricket field again. In the last game of the season he made 40 for the Players against the Gentlemen and he may well have been surprised, for he was an essentially modest man, at the warmth of the feeling which applauded his score.

Happily, pessimism was premature. For the next two seasons, after the end of the Eton half, Hirst came back into the Yorkshire side for at least a few matches. In 1920 his finest exploit was a score of 81 against Surrey at the Oval. In spite of this lusty effort, Yorkshire lost the game by 31 runs, a fate they might have avoided if Hirst had not been out to an outrageously acrobatic catch by Fender. In 1921 there were two genuinely Hirst-like efforts, each of which reminded those who saw them that the greatest of county cricketers had not forgotten the art of delighting his fellow-Yorkshiremen.

YORKSHIRE COUNTY CRICKETERS AT ONE OF
LORD HAWKE'S PARTIES AT WIGHILL PARK

Back row: J. T. Brown, W. Rhodes, R. Moorhouse, J. B. Wostinholm
(county sec.), Rev. E. J. Carter, Turner (scorer), Schofield Haigh;
Middle row: G. H. Hirst, J. Tunnicliffe, E. Wainwright; *Front row:*
F. Milligan, D. Hunter, Lord Hawke. D. Denton.

THREE FRIENDS AT
BRIGHTON

*Hirst and Rhodes are the
'great twin brethren'; with
their friend Schofield Haigh
they are the three musketeers.
Haigh was a magnificent
bowler, a gay humorist and
truly described as 'for eighteen
years the sunshine of the
Yorkshire eleven'.*

GEORGE HIRST IMMEDIATELY AFTER WORLD WAR I
'*Here was a man who might have sat back and smoked his pipe;
as it was, at forty-eight he batted like a gay youngster.*'

J. T. BROWN

JOHN TUNNICLIFFE

LORD HAWKE

SCHOFIELD HAIGH

DAVID DENTON

Five of the best at the best of periods

Hirst and Rhodes at Weston-Super-Mare, 1914, when Drake took ten wickets in an innings

(a) (b)

(a) *Relaxing at Festival Time;* (b) *Hirst speaking from the pavilion balcony at Scarborough during the Festival of 1921 when he retired from first-class cricket*

III

The last game of the north-country season was, by hallowed tradition, the Gentlemen *v.* Players match at Scarborough. There is always something nostalgic about that final game, as though players and spectators were revelling in the last glint of sunshine before winter and the soccer season set in.

With a pleasant gesture, the authorities made Hirst captain of the Players, and though he failed in the first innings he hit finely in the second, and then, with a final flourish, took the last two wickets. It was his fiftieth birthday and the crowd would not go home. Under the front of the pavilion they gathered, chanting: 'We want George Hirst, we want George Hirst.' Every member of that company was excited, uplifted, moved by the spontaneous warmth of the occasion. Emotional moments for Yorkshiremen are infrequent but intense. Finally a sturdy figure came out on to the balcony. The applause swelled and then died down. He bent forward, looking down, his hands on the rail in front of him. Never was his natural dignity, his absolute freedom from self-consciousness, plainer to see. His voice, when he spoke, was clear and firm.

'Ladies and gentlemen, I'd like to call you the cricketing public. I thank you for your kindness to me. A person always knows his limitations and I'm not such a good man as you make me out to be.' (Laughter, cheers and cries of 'Nay, George!')

'If I've had any broad views on what they call the game of life, I've learnt them on the cricket field. I've loved many games but I've been a bit more efficient at cricket. From an unselfish point of view, it's the best game.

'What can you have better than a nice green field, with the wickets set up, and to go out and do the best for your side? I leave first-class cricket to those who have got to come. I hope they'll have the pleasure in it that I have had.'

The huge crowd roared their affection for several minutes;

then they broke up into groups and very slowly melted away. He turned and walked into the room behind the balcony. The greatest of all county cricketers had gone into retirement.

Eight years later, at the age of fifty-eight, he was prevailed on, perhaps against his better judgement, to turn out once more in a Scarborough Festival match. He made one run and then Bowes, who was making his way as fast bowler, clean bowled him with a swift and deadly ball. As Hirst walked away he spoke to the bowler.

'A grand ball that, lad. I couldn't have played that one when I was good.'

CHAPTER NINE

What Manner of Cricketer?

*'Before a big ordeal he would be sitting smoking his old pipe
and beaming as though he was just going to have his dinner . . .'*

—Sir Jack Hobbs

I

GEORGE HIRST, most admirable of old soldiers, neither
died nor faded away. For the next seventeen years he was
coach at Eton College and also to the Yorkshire club.
During those years hundreds of boys and youths passed
through his hands, and there was not one of them, sophisticated member of 'Pop' or eager lad from a West Riding
mill town, who was not the gainer. Not every cricketer
makes an inspired coach and not every good coach has
necessarily been a fine cricketer. Hirst combined in his own
sturdy person all the qualities that make a superlative
coach: first, the respect-winning status due to supreme
attainment; then the knowledge and high technical skill
in the subject taught and the rare gift of imparting it; the
enthusiasm that comes from a deep love of the game, a
natural 'way' with young people, and, perhaps above all,
a passion to ensure that those who come afterwards shall
have every chance of doing even better what was done well
before. There are some who believe that coaching is everything; there are others who maintain that it merely curbs
and perhaps destroys a lad's natural abilities. Hirst's genius
in coaching (and the expression is not too strong) lay in
giving his pupil such fundamental groundwork as was
absolutely necessary and at the same time encouraging him
to develop his individual talent to the full within a framework of soundness and sense. With a pupil like Hedley

Verity, intelligent, receptive, ambitious, and consumingly
eager to learn, Hirst did wonders; but with a very different
type, George Macaulay, who was also highly intelligent, but
strongly individual and more than a little wayward, he also
did wonders. Verity, as all the world knows, became the
natural successor to Rhodes, and, though not quite as great
as his master, was a very fine bowler indeed. Yet, when he
first came under Hirst's eye, he was fastish and not nearly
so accurate as he afterwards became. In Macaulay, by some
remarkable gift of teaching, Hirst succeeded in laying a
foundation of first principles without seriously limiting his
pupil's fierily personal qualities.

Furthermore, as all his pupils would tell you, his generous
encouragement could make you play, if only to please him,
better than you ever thought you could. Consciously or
unconsciously, your style improved, and more than one
successful young player was heard to say: 'It wasn't me that
got the runs; it was George.' When Herbert Sutcliffe played
his first game for Yorkshire, Hirst was batting at the other
end. Dipper of Gloucestershire was bowling well outside the
off-stump and young Sutcliffe was completely baffled.
'Nay, Alf,' said Hirst, 'it's the lad's first game. Give him
something he can get at.' Dipper did nothing of the sort,
but Sutcliffe gained a confidence he never lost. When Hirst
had played in a team alongside a beginner, he had always
encouraged the lad into producing something better than
his previous best. So, in coaching, he brought out the very
best that was in a boy. He did not over-praise and, if it was
plain that you would 'never do', he would not in the end
fail to tell you, though he would tell you kindly.

Nothing illustrates the strength of Hirst's judgement
better than the careers of those two youthful aspirants,
Frank Dennis and Bill Bowes. Dennis was one of the best
young players who never quite made the established county
grade; Bowes went on to long county service and high Test

honours. Discussing the matter with Bowes long afterwards, Hirst said reflectively: 'Coaches' opinions often go wrong: look how wrong I was about you.'

It then transpired that Hirst had in the early days believed that Dennis would make a better bowler than Bowes. Yet never by any word or gesture that might have blighted the hopes of either lad, did Hirst express that opinion. No wonder Bowes said of him: 'I never hope to meet a better coach or a better man.'

He would jolly you along, and the only one to get the rough end of his tongue would be the one who was not trying his best. He once said to a very tall bowler who was not using his height to full advantage: 'Look at thee. Six foot high and balling out of t' backside of thi britches!'

He was something of a martinet in demanding from his pupils spotless flannels and a smart turn-out, holding that if you would not bother to look your best, you could hardly be relied on to *do* your best. Equipment, and especially boots, must be just right. Yet, characteristically, he would temper efficiency with mercy. Once a youngster on the M.C.C. staff was urgently sent for to do some bowling at the nets at Eton. The notice was short. His flannels were darkly grass-stained, his spare pair were at the cleaners, and he arrived with grubby flannels in his bag and perturbation in his heart.

'It's a bad do,' said Hirst, severe but kindly, 'but don't fret, lad. I'll show you how to cover those stains with chalk for the afternoon, but if you come here looking like that again, by gow . . .'

Whole generations of Yorkshiremen and Etonians have become better cricketers, and indeed better men, because they were coached by George Hirst. To the Yorkshiremen George Hirst's vernacular was their own form of expression and they understood it well; to the Etonians his vernacular was a strange, delightful language and they appreciated it

even more. In Yorkshire he was unquestionably accepted as
the typical, the model, almost the Creator's original sketch
for the Yorkshireman, and he was naturally at home with
such people. In the sophisticated world of Eton he suffered
no loss of equanimity. A youthful exquisite once accosted
him: 'Is it true, George, that you once made 2,000 runs and
took 200 wickets in a season?'

'That's right, sir.'

'Good God!' exclaimed the youth and strolled away.

And George Hirst survived even that.

Superficially, Eton and industrial Yorkshire differ in
many ways, yet they have some attributes in common.
Neither community exhibits emotions with ease and neither
is 'much given to idolatry'. Yet both will give praise, perhaps grudgingly at first but then wholeheartedly, where,
according to their widely different standards, they deem
praise to be due. Thus Yorkshire frankly adored George
Hirst, and so did Eton, too.

He adopted the Eton eleven just as he had adopted
Yorkshire and identified himself with its fortune. There was
a match in 1920 in which the powerful Winchester eleven
of Claude Ashton and Tom Raikes had cruelly trounced the
Eton bowling. During the usual post-mortem that follows
such misfortunes the Eton captain, a young gentleman
afterwards known as an excellent bowler in first-class cricket,
put the question to his professional adviser: 'Was there anything I did wrong, George?' (His figures that day had been
none for 86).

'Yes, sir,' replied George, 'I'll tell you what it was. You
bowled too long and you bowled too bad.'

There is a valedictory tale of his last summer at Eton
which, apocryphal or not, happily underlines the affection
in which the coach and the college held each other. It was
the final practice game before the Lord's match and Hirst
was bowling for the second eleven against the Eleven. The

captain of the Eleven, whose imagination was fertile and whose word was law, felt that a charming legend would be created if George could do the hat-trick in his very last game. He gave his instructions accordingly. The first batsman was caught, the second was bowled by a beauty and the third got himself out with such deft artistry that no one could have guessed that the thing was done on purpose. So, amid a hurricane of applause, George Hirst completed his hat-trick. No one ever discovered how the leakage occurred, but, though he knew the matter had been arranged, Hirst never revealed his knowledge by a word or a look. It was the most Eton-like gesture of his Etonian career.

When he retired from Eton, he was chief guest at a dinner at which the flower of Etonian cricket was present, and never were sentiments at a farewell dinner more sincerely felt and expressed. He was sixty-seven years old, but his eye was as bright as it had ever been. For another five years he still regularly played the game he loved in his home district and it was not until he was seventy-two that he retired from club cricket. Even then, till the time of his death, eleven years later still, there was not a day on which he did not talk of cricket wisely, happily, humorously, and with abiding affection.

II

This was George Herbert Hirst, the man who in a career of thirty years made over 36,000 runs and took more than 2,700 wickets, made 601 catches (550 of them for Yorkshire), did the double fourteen times, played in twenty-four Test matches, all but three of them against Australia, and was described by his most famous captain as the greatest county cricketer of all time.

He was one of the two greatest all-rounders in a period of great all-rounders. As a batsman he was not of the classic school of MacLaren or Fry, nor did he display the elegant artistry of Spooner or R. E. Foster, or quite the same eager, light-cavalry approach as his friend and contemporary, David Denton. Though a cavalier by nature, he was, in his attack with either bat or ball, more like one of Cromwell's russet-coated captains who knew what they did fight for and loved what they knew. He knew that he fought for Yorkshire and he loved Yorkshire with all his heart. His batting expressed his outward character: it was blunt, bold, honest, and immensely vigorous, and he was at his best in trouble. Just as Mark Tapley demanded a black outlook in order to be cheerful, so Hirst was a cricketer from whom impending disaster struck bright and cheerful sparks. He could, on the occasions when pure defence was needful, defend his wicket with north-country dourness, but far oftener peril spurred him into the attack. Time and time again he would come in, with Yorkshire in grave jeopardy, and, by the time he was out, his county were on their way to victory. If ever there was a natural match-winning cricketer, it was George Hirst.

He could hit all round the wicket, but his favourite strokes were hard straight drives on the on-side or several varieties of daring pull, very much in the manner of Patsy Hendren at a later date. This pull of Hirst's was as characteristic of the man as was Ranji's leg-glance or Palairet's off-drive, and knowledgeable spectators would go a long way to see it. He was quick of foot and eye and anyone who willingly fielded in the square-leg area against him could be suspected of suicidal tendencies. The foundations of his batting were power, courage, and a conviction that a bat was an attacking weapon. His tremendous pulling, though potent, was scarcely elegant, and he was capable of going down on his right knee and savagely propelling the ball to or over the square-leg boundary with a stroke that was half Jessop and half village blacksmith. There is a story of Hirst in an early game at Lord's scoring a rapid 50 by methods

forceful but unorthodox. This brought snorts of disapproval
from an elderly top-hatted gentleman in the pavilion who
exclaimed at intervals:

'Disgraceful! Shocking! Look at the fellow's feet!'

'Ay,' interrupted a Yorkshire voice, 'but look at t'
scoreboard!'

III

Much has been written about Hirst's bowling. He began,
we are told, as an ordinary bread-and-butter young bowler
with a nice quick action, a straight up-and-downer, as
Rhodes called it. In a sense this is true, but, if he was an
ordinary bowler, he must have been one of the best 'ordinary'
bowlers who ever broke into county cricket. His figures
before the coming of the famous swerve were good enough to
prove this. It is easier to repeat what baffled batsmen said
about it than to describe what actually happened. Its victims said that it would come at you like a fast throw-in from
cover-point. The ball, delivered in combination with a
cross-wind, or better still with a diagonal head-wind, would
swing in the air and completely bamboozle the batsman.
You could watch his left shirt-sleeve slipping down as he
bowled the ball and you could see him thoughtfully rolling
it up again as he walked back to begin his run for the next
one. In between you were not so sure. Generally the delivery was very fast, but occasionally there was a slow ball
which baffled the poor batsman even more, because he had
finished his stroke before the ball arrived, and clean bowled
him. There had been swerving bowlers before, like Barton
King, the most famous of Philadelphian cricketers, and
Albert Trott, the Middlesex Australian, who was Hirst's
contemporary and practised by bowling round a large box
in front of the wicket, but Hirst's swerve was more deadly
and more frequent than that of either. (Trott's box, he
always said, was George Giffen's bat and if he couldn't

swerve past it he could beat it with an off-break.) Hirst was, to the best of my knowledge, the first bowler regularly to have three men fielding close in on the leg-side, on the chance of an induced mishit. When the ball came swerving across from the off at the last instant, he must have been as hard to play as the most difficult of modern bowlers. Imagination boggles at the thought of what he would have done with the specialized leg-trap policemen of today.

As a fieldsman, his reputation, both for courage and complete reliability, was of the highest. Only Woolley, W.G., and two or three others have taken a greater number of catches, and it is without the least disrespect to such remarkable close-wicket fielders of today as Lock, Trueman, Stewart, and Vic Wilson to say that almost every catch taken by Hirst was from a full-blooded drive, either at mid-off or off his own bowling, and this in a period when the off-drive was the batsman's joy and pride. Today that stroke is, to say the least of it, rarer than it once was, though we saw it as long as Sir Leonard Hutton was playing; in Hirst's day the off-drive came like a jet-propelled rocket. The question may still be asked: what happens when an irresistible force meets an immovable object? The answer is that the force ceased to be completely irresistible, and that the immovable object was a large powerful hand, hard as iron and yet wholly adhesive, and that the astonished batsman was out, caught Hirst. All Hirst's catches were bravely taken in front of the wicket. Of all the gallant 600 catches, I doubt if there were six dollies among the lot.

CHAPTER TEN

The Man in the Round

'What can you have better than a nice green field, with the wickets up, and to go out and do the best for your side?'
—George Herbert Hirst

I

As we have seen, after leaving Eton Hirst still enjoyed himself in club cricket and it was not until he was seventy-two that he finally called it a day. Living in his own house in his own town of Huddersfield he was a familiar figure in that sometimes foggy but always virile town; he was seen at many of Yorkshire's home games, at Headingley Test matches, and at the three annual games of the Scarborough Festival. In every pavilion in England he was a welcome guest; if he walked round a Yorkshire ground, his movement was a kind of royal progress. At least three generations of cricketers greeted him, and the crowds cheered him, somewhat to the embarrassment of his family, as he took his seat in front of the pavilion. He had that gift, normally a royal prerogative, of being able to accept a kind of adulation without either being puffed up or embarrassed; his natural dignity and courtesy were proof against his ever being anything but what he was: George Herbert Hirst, a plain, honest Yorkshireman, who had had the good fortune to possess high skill in a happy, vigorous game. He had, to the highest degree, the virtue that the Victorians called manliness, but without a jot of Victorian sententiousness. To peer, industrialist, working man or timid schoolboy he was always the same: a friendly soul, kindly but sensible, whose genial face, without the least affectation, radiated to the full the happy spirit of the English game. One of the younger 'old hands' at Kirkheaton told me: 'When we were young lads we used to nip out of Sunday School to catch a glimpse of George Herbert. Regular as clockwork he used to come over by bus to see his mother and he'd come swinging along with his trilby hat and rolled umbrella, smart as a new pin. To see him smile—and he always *would* smile—used to set us kids up for the week.'

Walking in his own town in later years, he was a venerable figure; not in the conventional sense of the word, for not until he was eighty did he begin to look really slight or frail: he was venerable in the sense that he was revered (and deserved to be revered) by all who knew him. He never forgot a friend and he counted his friends in every part of the world where cricket was played. His thoughts seldom strayed far from cricket, and if he saw the grubbiest of small boys playing their first games on the grassy edge of the road he would watch them with grave appraisal and then say:

'Now hold it this way, lad.'

While he had charm and friendliness, he was never lacking in shrewdness and sharp humour. His enjoyment in all departments of the game was deep and strong. 'When you're both a batter and a bowler,' he once told me, 'you enjoy yourself twice as much.'

II

Like W.G., Hirst found that anecdotes gathered round him. Some were true in fact; those that were aprocryphal were true in spirit. He was naturally generous in praise of what he believed to be a fine effort. After an innings by the fragile and delicate-looking P. F. Warner, which showed high art and courage, Hirst exclaimed: 'By, Mr Warner, if you'd had a stomach like me or Schofield, you'd have been a champion!'

In the Grenadier Guards before the 1914-18 War was a

bandsman from Kirkheaton named Harry Stead. While he was watching Yorkshire play Surrey at the Oval, a message arrived at his home, ordering him to return to barracks for a regimental parade. His wife was at her wits end to know how to communicate with him: at last she sent off a telegram to George Hirst at the Oval begging him to help. The telegram was brought out to Hirst at mid-off. 'Sitha,' he said to the telegraph-boy, 'go round the boundary and whenever you see a soldier in a red coat, ask him if his name's Harry and if it is tell him to get off home like billyho.' That is how Bandsman Stead paraded in time. 'And,' added Hirst solemnly, as he told me the story, 'if two other chaps called Harry went running home to their missuses it wouldn't do 'em any harm.'

His conduct on the field was founded on a principle of absolute right. All who played with him, and especially those who kept wicket to him and were in the best position to judge, maintained that he was scrupulously fair in his appeals and would never claim a leg-before unless he was completely sure he was justified. I have myself seen him him hold up the ball to the umpire to show that what looked like a legitimate catch had in fact touched the ground first. He did this without fuss, because he was incapable of any action that was not frank and open-hearted. He would do the fair thing, it was said of him, because it was right, not because it did not matter. His generosity on the field never slid into anything that might wrongly have given a point away; that is to say, he was capable of a generous gesture at his own expense, but not at the expense of his side. He once bowled Warren Bardsley first ball. In the second innings the first ball Bardsley received from Hirst was a full toss and gratefully he pushed it round to fine-leg for three. This brought him to the bowler's end and he was genuinely grateful to the veteran for having given him an innocuous ball to break his pair.

'Thanks,' said Bardsley.

'Don't thank me,' said Hirst, 'it were t'ball that slipped.'

A bowler who was later to be an England captain was bowling at Scarborough. For some reason he lost his equanimity and delivered a cartload of bumpers. Hirst, who was umpiring, looked stern. At the end of the over he said to the offender, handing him his sweater:

'Put this on and go away until you can behave yourself.'

It was a rebuke from Sinai, and the sinner, to his eternal credit, accepted it as such.

He once told me how F. S. Jackson, who was standing as a candidate in a Leeds municipal election, asked him to speak for him. Hirst laughed as he repeated his 'speech'.

' "Ladies and gentlemen," I said. "Mr Jackson's a fine man and a grand cricketer, but if you get him on to this Council, he'll play less cricket, and that'll be a bad thing for Yorkshire, England and everybody. So don't vote for him, any of you!" Mr Jackson—Sir Stanley as he was later —had a real good laugh over that.'

Lord Hawke said that 'George's smile went right round his head and met at the back'. Near-poets celebrated it as a 'square-cut smile'. It was with this sort of smile that he wrote to a youthful admirer: 'Dear Willie, You asked for my autograph. Here are two—one for yourself and one for a swop. Yours sincerely, G. H. Hirst.' It was this sort of smile that I saw when, at least fifty years after the event, he told me that sad story of Bobby Peel. It happened, I think, at Chesterfield and George Hirst was having breakfast in the professionals' modest hotel before setting off for the ground to begin the match. To him staggered in Bobby Peel in what Hirst, as he unfolded the narrative, paradoxically described as 'a proper condition'. Peel at the time had two major interests: one was cricket, the other was less reputable. A fine forcing bat and Yorkshire's best slow bowler before

Rhodes, Peel had a strong weakness for the bottle, not merely in the evening, which is allowable within reason, but occasionally in the morning, which is inconvenient for all concerned. George Hirst, the kindliest and most tolerant of men, was not censorious, but he was deeply concerned lest his colleague should be, as he called it, 'caught in the act', and thus bring disgrace on himself and on the team. At all costs Bobby must be got back to bed. At first cajolingly and then forcefully, but always with good temper, Hirst propelled his charge upstairs, undressed him in the most comradely manner, and put him to bed. This deed of mercy completed, Hirst hurried to the ground, changed, and sought audience with his captain.

'I'm sorry, my lord,' he said; 'Peel's apologies and he's been taken very queer in the night and won't be able to turn out this morning.'

Lord Hawke expressed sincere sympathy, as he always did with his professionals, and promised to come along and see the invalid in the evening. He then called for the twelfth man and, having lost the toss, led his men into the field. As they converged upon the middle Hirst saw with dawning dismay that there were not eleven fieldsmen present but twelve. There, his face red, his cap awry, the ball in his hand, stood Bobby Peel, in an even 'properer' condition than before. Hirst told me that he simply dared not glance in Lord Hawke's direction: he merely heard him say:

'Leave the field at once, Peel.'

'Not at all, my lord,' replied Bobby with respectful cheerfulness; 'I'm in fine form this morning.'

Whereupon he turned away from the wicket, solemnly took his run up, and delivered an elaborately cunning ball in the direction of the sightscreen. I am not precisely clear as to what happened next, but I imagine Peel was then led quietly away and that few people realized that a serious breach of discipline had occurred. In the evening Hirst found the delinquent sleeping it off and in the morning he was truculent.

'You must write an apology to his lordship at once,' said Hirst.

'That I never will.'

'Then you're finished, Bobby.'

'Niver i' this world,' retorted Peel; 'they'll have to send for me; they can't do without me.'

Hirst argued, stormed, pleaded, but vainly.

'And, of course,' he told me, 'his lordship sent for him all right, but only to give him the sack officially, and who was the sorriest out of us three, I wouldn't like to say. As for not being able to do without him, Bobby was fairly dropped on, because, as you'll remember, Wilfred came along the very next season. Yorkshire were lucky. But Lord Hawke was for ever sorry that Bobby had to go, and when they met later, at Scarborough and such places, they were the best of friends, and neither of them said a word against the other. But Bobby was never allowed to come back.'

Hirst told me the story in such a manner as revealed a good deal of his true character. He did not moralize; he did everything possible to honour his loyalty both to his club and to his delightful but unreliable companion; he was sorry for the dismissal, though he reckoned it inevitable; he was delighted that Lord Hawke and Bobby should eventually make friends; and finally, when the thing ceased to be a tragedy, he could laugh at his own unsuccessful efforts to prevent poor Bobby from committing cricket suicide. His laugh was delightful, and it was easy to see how in the old days it had made despondent colleagues feel that the world was not such a bad place. And his method of telling the story showed that, as Lord Hawke always maintained, he was a remarkable raconteur in the West Riding vernacular.

One story he told me himself was about Schofield Haigh's inveterate habit of practical joking. Once, going into a ground on which the county had never played before, Schofield spoke in a mysterious whisper to the gate-man.

'Don't look now,' said Schofield, 'but there's a man been following us. Suffers from delusions, poor chap. Thinks he's a cricketer, and calls himself George Hirst. Don't let him in, I'm warning you.'

'And naturally,' Hirst told me, 'when I came up a bit later, he wouldn't let me in.'

'And what did you do?'

Hirst's laugh was musical and merry.

'I said to him, "All right, then, if I'm not George Hirst, I'm not. But if not, you go and tell his lordship he'll be a man short." '

His ultimate gift was the rare one of growing old gracefully, and those who only met him in his later days were impressed by his gentleness and could not quite recognize the tremendous dynamo of energy, of pulsing vitality this frail old gentleman had once been. This quiet and serene quality represented the final mellowing and blending of his integrity, his sense of rightfulness and fair play. From youth to age he was a man without malice. To the end of his days he would always eagerly inquire how the young entry was shaping.

'Well,' his successor at Headingley would reply; 'we've Plink, who can spin 'em from the off, and Plonk, who turns 'em from leg, and Plunk, who can conceal a googly till the last minute.'

'Ah,' said George, 'but have you got anybody who can bowl straight?' Nobody ever played straighter.

As a little-known author has said: 'There were great cricketers before; there are great cricketers now, and, happily, there will be great cricketers again. But in the history of the game George Herbert Hirst will always hold his own shining place, a romantic but essentially robust figure. A noble game is the nobler because he played it, and to every lad he taught, to every man who knew him, from Kirkheaton to Melbourne, from Sydney to Lord's, he will ever remain the revered master and the living inspiration.'

CHAPTER ELEVEN

New Star Rising

'Rhodes emerged as a star of the very first magnitude right from the start.'—H. S. Altham

I

THERE HAS never been such a career in cricket as that of Wilfred Rhodes. Not even W. G. Grace, unchallengeably named 'the great cricketer', was the hero of so remarkable a success story. By comparison the industrious apprentice was a shiftless fellow. The purpose of these pages is to show a man who at the age of twenty-one took 154 wickets in his first county season and went in at No. 11 for England in his second; joined in a record last-wicket Test stand against Australia; went forward to go in first with Hobbs (the greatest batsman of his time), and joined with this pre-eminent partner in a first-wicket stand which remained a record for thirty-six years. Nor was this the end, or anything like it. After the first World War, at the age of forty-two, he turned once more to his old love and became for several seasons the undisputed leader of English bowling, and finally, a couple of months before his forty-ninth birthday, he reappeared on the international scene and by a characteristic bowling performance played a vital part in bringing back the Ashes into England's possession after fourteen years. For four seasons more he was a valued player and strategist in his county side. When he retired at the age of fifty-three, he had scored just under 40,000 runs and taken over 4,000 wickets. With his first ball in Australia he took a wicket and with his last ball in first-class cricket, also against the Australians, he got his man. It was his final nail in the coffin of the common enemy: the last moment of thirty-two years of pure relentless purpose.

II

In August 1958 I sat beside him at Bournemouth, watching Yorkshire play Hampshire. He was eighty years old, but his face was full, round, and unwrinkled, and his complexion was as fresh and clear as a boy's. I watched with my eyes; Wilfred Rhodes watched with his ears, with his unrivalled knowledge and experience, and with a kind of sixth sense which told him more about what was technically happening than my eyes told me. There was not a sound of bat on ball or a burst of applause for a boundary, a clever stop by a fieldsman or the fall of a wicket, which did not seize and hold his interest through his imagination. His quickfire of question was like a machine gun. 'What's he doing now? Where did he pitch that one? What's he dropping 'em short for?' There was nothing that escaped his unseeing gaze.

That blindness should overtake those keen blue eyes is in itself a tragedy difficult to express in words. Long before he suffered this terrible loss a neighbour was congratulating him on his remarkable eyesight. 'Is it true, Wilfred, that when you had been batting for some time in your great stands with Jack Hobbs, you could see the seam on the ball?'

'That's right,' replied Wilfred blandly, 'but you should have played with Ranji; he could see the stitches.'

Through the years he has borne his affliction with the greatest patience and the highest courage.

Sometimes a sly humour underlines this courage. After the Leeds Test of 1956 Rhodes was travelling home with his daughter in a compartment crowded with people who were excitedly discussing the game. One of them glanced at the quiet figure in the corner seat and whispered sympathetically to the lady with him.

'Is he your dad?'

'Yes.'

'Blind, isn't he?'

'Yes.'

'I wonder if he knows anything about cricket?'

'A bit.'

'Fine. You ought to take him to a match or two and explain things to him. It would do him a world of good to have an interest.'

'And there was I in my corner,' said Rhodes, as he told me the tale, '*and I never cried squeak.*'

All through the years of his affliction he has never 'cried squeak'.

At first his disability was comparatively slight and it came upon him toward the end of the season following his retirement from first-class cricket. This was during the summer of 1931, which he spent with the Perth Club.

'I never meant to go to Perth,' he told me, 'but the men they sent to fetch me told me they'd stop all night in my house and all the next day, too, till I promised to go with them.

'It was after that season that I had to give up the game,' he went on. 'It was the beginning of my eye trouble. I found that a straight full toss could bowl me any time.'

During the last ten years, instead of playing, he has 'watched' cricket with keen intelligence, enjoying what was good and being severely critical of what he felt to be feeble or inefficient. Never for a moment has he lost his interest in the game or his habit of measuring the player's fallibility against his own Everest-like standard of perfection. (He told me that nobody nowadays could make a proper on-drive, except Peter May.) On that sunny afternoon at Bournemouth—a golden day in a dank summer—he went into the visitors' dressing-room and talked to Yorkshire's new slow bowler, Don Wilson, a lanky left-handed lad, who had had considerable success with the second eleven and some success with the first.

'Well, how are you going on, lad?'

'Not too bad,' says Wilson with the mingled modesty of one who knows he has a lot to learn and the confidence of one who means to have a good go at learning it.

'What bothers you most?'

'I'm fairly all right on length, but not so hot on direction.'

'Well, you know what that means,' said Rhodes; 'it means practice and practice *and* practice.'

Back in our seats we watched the cricket again. His voice was gruff, though not so gruff as it used to be, and his critical faculty did not wholly exclude praise: 'That sounded fairly sweet off the bat. Is that Burnet's fifty?' And then more austerely: 'How does the chap expect to get wickets if he piches 'em as short as that?'

III

His father, a serious, bearded man and a keen cricketer, cut out a pitch on the grass near their farm-cottage home for Wilfred to bat and bowl on. (All his life he has remained a countryman.) The paternal coaching went on all the winter. 'I got hold of an old ball,' Rhodes told me, 'and rubbed it with chalk, so that I could watch whether it was spinning or not. Then I bowled against the woodshed door, and kept on.'

That persistence was one secret of Rhodes's success. He kept on. The lad went to school in the neighbouring parish of Hopton, and when he left it he was put to his first job on the railway. (This was at the neighbouring small town of Mirfield, which has produced some remarkable cricketers as well as remarkable theologians.) It is matter for the consideration of educational theorists that, whereas his formal education did not extend much farther than this period at the village school, he is today, at over eighty, a widely cultivated man, with a knowledge of the wider world and a breadth of interests by no means confined to games. He has this in common with Sir Donald Bradman, that he has never taken up any interest without an overwhelming determination to master it. He would conquer knowledge by sheer application as he conquered batsmen.

There is no record that he languished in artistic frustration during his short period in the engine sheds at Mirfield station. No doubt he got on with his job. His main trouble was that while his duties finished at two o'clock on Saturday afternoon he had all his work cut out to get back to Kirkheaton in order to start cricket at half-past two. Sometimes he walked, with that brisk, economical step which we saw later in his approach to the wicket, and sometimes, if a job finished late, he ran all the way. I can think of only W.G. himself (or perhaps John Small) who would have travelled so far and so fast on his own two feet to make sure of a game of cricket. With the Old Man, of course, there was an added exuberance; with young Rhodes it was absolute determination. Even so, this long walk (or gallop) from duty to pleasure seemed in time to become too much of a good thing, and one Saturday he took it upon himself to ring the two o'clock knocking-off bell at one-thirty. That ended his railway career and when he received an offer from a Scottish club to become a professional cricketer in their service he accepted cheerfully. It was a long way from home for a Yorkshire lad to go, but at least he wouldn't have to run to the ground every Saturday.

In one especial sense he was not so far from home, for the people of the Border towns are not dissimilar in character and industry from those of the West Riding. Both peoples are sturdy individualists, kindly at heart but suspicious of the incomer until they have admitted him to their circles, and given to near-religious fanaticisms in support of their favourite game. Indeed, a tolerant Borderer will concede in the kindest way that a Yorkshireman is not so bad; he is merely a Scot of second quality. The comparison, naturally, applies both ways. The industrial link between the two is wool and the magnificent tweed cloth into which it is manufactured. Every time that young Rhodes walked from his lodgings to the Galashiels cricket ground on the wind-swept hill-side of Mossilee, he passed the end of a Huddersfield Street.

If a biographer may insert a mildly irrelevant paragraph, I should say that for me Galashiels is an enchanted town: it was the home town of my father and grandfather, a minister there for over fifty years; it has not only its own Gala Water but the loveliest river in Britain, the Tweed; it is close to Sir Walter Scott's Abbotsford; and, of course, for two years it possessed Wilfred Rhodes.

He spent the two seasons of 1896 and '97 at Galashiels, going in to bat first and bowling a fast-medium ball. ('What they call a "seamer" today,' he told me.) An elderly relative of mine, one of the Galashiels old guard, would repeat to his dying day: 'Ah, it was in Gala that we *taught* Wilfred Rhodes how to play cricket.' And when sixty years had passed since this reputed period of education Rhodes could say with a smile: 'Whenever they send me a Border paper, they never forget to rub it in to this day.' His stay in Galashiels ended amicably, mainly as the result of a conversation with A. G. Grant Asher, a well-known Scottish cricketer and still more famous Rugby footballer, who was then president of the Grange, Scotland's leading club. Grant Asher said: 'There's nothing for a player of your calibre in Scotland. Go back to Yorkshire, where they take the game seriously.'

Rhodes was a young man who took the game very seriously indeed. He was soon back in Yorkshire and agreeing to stay. There is a story that Yorkshire might easily have lost him, because Warwickshire officials were on his track and only missed him by one day. The same tale is recounted

of Hedley Verity, but it is nearly impossible for a Yorkshireman to think of these two giants as another county's near-
misses. If there had not been a Yorkshire for Rhodes and
Verity to play for, it would have had to be invented to give
them their background. Following the excellently practical
Yorkshire custom, Rhodes was allocated to one of the clubs
within the county. Sheffield United was the club chosen for
him, but he had been with them only two days when he
was given his chance to appear in the county side. So, as a
kindly observer noted, there appeared in the Yorkshire
team 'a new face, pleasant, ruddy, with eyes of a wonderful
blue.'[1] The honour, if well deserved, was high. He was
picked to play for Yorkshire in their opening match against
M.C.C. at Lord's. There is a legend that Rhodes and another bowler named Cordingley took part in this southern
tour on trial. In the M.C.C. match, which was the first of
their games, Rhodes bowled so well that at the end of it
Cordingley packed his bag, shook hands in sportsmanlike
fashion, and went back to Yorkshire without finishing the
tour. The only thing against the story is that it can hardly
be true. Cordingley, who was a good bowler but not a
genius, had a trial for Yorkshire later and then played a
season with Sussex. Lord Hawke has said that, despite the
pleasing legend, he had never even from the beginning had
the slightest doubt about Rhodes's superiority at every point.

Batting at No. 8, Rhodes scored 4 and 16; in the first
innings he took two wickets for 39 and in the second four for
24. The M.C.C. side was a strong one and the batsmen
Rhodes dismissed—the famous Albert Trott was the first—
were all seasoned players, but what impressed everyone
most was his beautiful, easy action and his puzzling variety
in flight. When he retired thirty-two years later his action
was still beautiful and his flight was still puzzling.

In his second game, against Somerset at Bath, he started

[1] *Cricket Memories* by a Country Vicar.

off on that career of devastation that was to last so long. On a treacherous pitch he took seven for 24 and then six for 24. (Somerset's second innings total was 35.) It was a season ideal for a slow left-hand bowler, a time of mixed weather when wet pitches seemed to be for ever drying under a hot sun, and Rhodes took the most cunning advantage of every variation. That imposing feature of the Yorkshire county year-book, modestly called *Exceptional Bits of Bowling*, credits Rhodes with nearly fifty such 'bits'. The somewhat austere compiler of this list does not seem to have found anything at all exceptional in Rhodes's first season. Yet in Yorkshire's victory over Surrey at Bradford he took six for 46 and then, aided in the second innings by some spectacular stumping by David Hunter, seven for 24.

So the trail of '98 went on: with a five for 33 and four for 34 against Leicestershire; eleven for 94 against Essex; six for 32 against Notts; and, winding up with the M.C.C. game at Scarborough, five for 59. In Yorkshire they are reluctant to over-praise the young and, after admitting that a legitimate successor to Peate and Peel might possibly be on the way, there was a tendency to hedge: 'Ah, yes, pretty good, but, after all, this season's glue-pot pitches have handed him his 154 wickets on a plate. Wait and see what he does next year.'

IV

No one need have worried. The summer of 1899 was a reasonably dry one and gave slow left-hand bowlers little obvious assistance. When, by skill and good fortune, he could extract anything from the pitch he took full advantage. On the strength of his last, that is, his first season's, performance, he was named as one of *Wisden's* five Cricketers of the Year; a rare honour indeed. I can think of only one other bowler who was so early heralded as a Cricketer of the Year: this was Bob Appleyard, who, fifty-two years later, took 200 wickets in his first season. Rhodes's bag in 1899, this season of batsmen's wickets, was bigger than what he had captured before: 179 instead of 154. At Bath against Somerset he took five for 11 and was described as 'unplayable'; in the next game at Bristol he took six for 16 and then three for 15 on a wicket by no means heaven-sent for slow bowlers. When he did eventually find a wicket to his liking, the effect was truly sensational. At Leyton he was more difficult to play than he had ever been before and, if his five for 11 at Bath was 'unplayable', what were the Essex batsmen to make of nine for 28? With F. S. Jackson he bowled unchanged right through the match and finished with a total booty of fifteen wickets at less than four and a half runs apiece.

Among his most creditable performances on unsuitably hard wickets were seven for 147 against Middlesex at Lord's and, on the small ground at Harrogate, five for 57, though it is only fair to say that he took heavy punishment in the second innings from Fry and Ranjitsinhji. No more than any other first-class bowler was he completely exempt from punishment, but punishment taught him patience and, in any event, he usually had the last laugh. When he played in his first Gentlemen v. Players match at Lord's, Fry 'went after him' again and, in company with W.G., belted him all over the field. W.G. had a good reason for this lively display. It is not often that a man makes 78 within a few days of his fifty-first birthday. But for Rhodes it was a landmark. He had bowled against Grace, the greatest of all cricketers. More than thirty years later he would bowl at Bradman, the next greatest. Between these two Titans the career of Wilfred Rhodes spanned the years like a triumphal arch.

Rhodes in this season entered on a Test career which was to last in rich variety for twenty-seven years. His first Test at Nottingham was W.G.'s last. This was the game after which the Old Man, though he had not failed conspicuously with the bat, felt that he ought to retire from Test cricket. ('It's no use, Charlie, my hands are too far from the ground.') Rhodes's bowling figures—four for 58 and three for 60— showed that he had bowled steadily, if with no more penetration than anyone else; in the second Test his analysis of three for 108 against a powerful batting side did not flatter him: in fact, it underrated him, failing to show the artful tenacity with which he fought the first of his many duels with that smiling cavalier of the bat, Victor Trumper. Which of the two would eventually meet his match only history could show.

CHAPTER TWELVE

Golden Era

'Wilfred Rhodes . . . occupies a solitary and splendid niche in the temple of fame.'—H. S. Altham

I

THE YEAR 1900 was the first in that glorious triennium during which Yorkshire reigned supreme over English cricket. Their batting was good and their fielding was relentless, but what kept them in pride upon the mountain-top was undoubtedly the matchless strength of their bowling. Their attack was not so much a spearhead as a trident, whose three prongs were three remarkable bowlers: in 1900, Rhodes and Haigh; in 1901, Rhodes and Hirst; and in 1902, Rhodes and Haigh again. Until we come to the Surrey attack half a century later, there has never been an attack like it. In the three years these three took between them, in the first year, 486 wickets; in the second, 490; in the third, 454; and, out of this fantastic total of 1,430, Rhodes's share was 725. In each of these seasons he captured well over 200 wickets and he achieved this partly through his supreme skill and partly through his own brand of steely determination. He willed, more than any other bowler, to take 200 wickets. In the first three weeks of the 1900 season he actually took fifty wickets in half a dozen games. In both 1900 and 1901 he took his hundredth wicket by 21st June.

Contemporary accounts ransack a whole thesaurus of epithets in striving to describe his destructive powers: among the adjectives on view were: deadly, irresistible, unplayable, havoc-wreaking. In match after match he 'took the chief honours', 'routed the enemy', 'carried all before him'. The Yorkshire year-book confines its list of his 'exceptional bits' of Yorkshire bowling to seven for 20 against Worcestershire and eight for 23 against Hampshire. This is a narrow view, presupposing that such feats as eight for 68, seven for 72, eight for 43 on a 'great day' against Lancashire, seven for 33 and eight for 28 were in no way exceptional—for Wilfred Rhodes. And the supposition was correct. Everything that happened in Rhodes's season must have seemed monotonous to the scorers and a bad dream for the batsmen.

On the other hand, there were moments when he met foemen who bravely resisted the irresistible. In both games against Sussex he bowled with no less than his usual power and accuracy, but found the princely Ranjitsinhji in the kind of royal mood which turned the most masterly bowlers into peasants and serfs. In three innings of the two games Ranji made 72, 87, and 87 again, the majority of the runs joyfully scored off Rhodes's bowling. Yet Rhodes did not falter under pressure; sticking imperturbably to his task, he survived the ordeal to finish with nine for 141 in the first game and seven for 115 in the second. It was cavalier treatment meted out to a fighting roundhead, but Rhodes at least showed that he could take it as well as hand it out.

There was even more banging about in the tremendous tussle with Gloucestershire, which, despite a dazzling 100 by Jessop in each innings, Yorkshire won by 40 runs. Jessop's frequent firework displays constituted something never seen in cricket before or since. The only thing to be compared with them was a Brock's benefit. Jessop was no mere slogger, but a hitter of scientific and controlled power, and he ruled the bowlers with a rod of iron. Rhodes, along with his fellow-sufferers, received a terrible mauling. Yet his final figures—eight for 72 and six for 120—were a monument to his fortitude and endurance. Two legends have come down from this titanic battle. Hirst's batting efforts did not quite equal Jessop's tale of two centuries, but he came remarkably near to doing so with 111 and 92.

'Why, George,' said an admirer, 'you did nearly as well as Mr Jessop.'

'No,' replied Hirst with judicial and characteristic fair-mindedness, 'his was against good bowling.'

Rhodes told me long years afterwards how he and his friends had plotted to curb Jessop's violence and how in this astonishing game the plot went wrong.

'Jessop was a terror,' he chuckled, 'and he'd tanned us so hard in the match before we reckoned in this game we'd make him go and fetch 'em. So we bowled wide on the offside. He fetched 'em all right. He went off like a spring-trap and, before you'd seen his feet move, he was standing on the offside of his stumps, pulling 'em over the square-leg boundary. After the tanning he gave us that day, we made up our minds we'd never let him fetch 'em again, it was too expensive. Ever afterwards we bowled so tight he never put up a big score against us again. No. I'm wrong. There *was* once. But I hardly like to tell you about that one.'

II

As the next year's spring came in with attendant sunshine, the pundits shook their heads again: 'It was all very well in 1900, when the pitches were made for him like mud-pies, but what will he do now on these billiard-table wickets?'

The answer was simple. Rhodes did just the same. He had taken more than 250 wickets before; he took 250 wickets again. He had done well in the decently dry summer of two years before. On the perfect wickets of 1901 his remorseless length and puzzling flight saved him from severe punishment; when the sun shone after rare showers and he received even the tiniest help, he bowled as though the pitch were deplorable; and when, as will occasionally happen in the driest of seasons, the pitch *had* in fact become deplorable, he did not so much dismiss the enemy as demolish them. At Trent Bridge, on an acknowledged brute of a wicket, the bowling figures in the Notts first innings of 13 were:

	Overs	Mdns	Runs	Wkts
Rhodes . .	7.5	4	4	6
Haigh . .	7	2	8	4

Six wickets for four runs. That was the story when the wicket played into his hands, but, in normal conditions, such as prevailed on the county's opening tour in the West Country, he was satisfied with no less than twenty-six wickets in two matches and right through the season his usual levy upon an innings ranged from five to seven. Sometimes his share of the booty was bigger, as against Middlesex at Lord's (eight for 53) and against Kent at Canterbury (eight for 50) and seldom was it less. Even when the gods fought against him his counter-attack was courageous. In the historic match with Somerset—Sammy Woods's 'champagne' match— Yorkshire's solitary defeat was certainly not Rhodes's fault. In the first innings he took five for 39 and in the second, when the Somerset batsmen sadistically piled on the agony up to a total of 630 runs, he retrieved from the wreckage figures of six for 145.

There was a similar happening in the Gentlemen v. Players game at Hastings, except that the order of achievement was reversed. On the first day against a batting side of immense strength Rhodes battled through to take six wickets for 132, but in the second innings the Gentlemen were ordered by W.G., their captain, to force the pace. Obediently they got themselves out and allowed Rhodes to return figures of six for 27.

Moreover, just to prove that this superlative bowler was himself human, his analysis suffered cruelly in the last game of the season, the Champion County v. the Rest match.

There he met his old enemy Jessop and was himself sorely stricken. There may or may not be a touch of poetic justice in the thought of the slaughterer being led to the slaughter, but Jessop fell upon the bowling as a hurricane sometimes falls upon some luckless Caribbean island, leaving nought but havoc in its wake. His score was 233, made in less than two and a half hours, and when he had finished his fell work on Rhodes, that patient, persistent bowler had to be content with three wickets for 179. This was the game about which he said humorously fifty-seven years later: 'I'd rather not tell you about that one.'

In spite of this parting fusillade, he headed the first-class bowling tables and that last punishing game did not topple him.

III

In many ways 1902 was one of the fullest and richest seasons in cricket history: it was certainly one of the wettest, and it saw a dramatically successful Australian tour, illumined in splendour by the batting of Trumper; it also contained two of the most sensational of all Test matches, whose memory has remained golden for well over half a century. Furthermore, there were at least two performances by Yorkshire bowlers which were not merely beyond praise but virtually beyond belief. And, as a final touch of fantasy, Rhodes finished the Test series with a batting average, buttressed by six not-outs, of 67, while the magnificent masters, Ranji and Fry, averaged 4.75 and 1.25.

Of the deeds of noble note which Hirst and Rhodes performed in combination I have already spoken and shall speak in a later chapter; the individual exploits of Rhodes furnish enough drama to be going on with. The season was so wet that, since he had taken over 250 wickets in the dry, unhelpful summer of 1901, his admirers confidently expected him to exact an even heavier tribute. When he in fact took some thirty wickets less, they were a little shocked. This young bowler had set himself such a fantastically high standard that a tally of 216 wickets in a wet year was reckoned not good enough. The fact is: the pitches were often so soaked that they did not dry quickly enough to be treacherous, remaining dead rather than difficult. Yet he took 216 wickets.

Yorkshire started their season at Lord's against an able M.C.C. eleven and, though they scored fewer than 200 runs, this total was enough to bring them victory by an innings and 70 runs. In M.C.C.'s first innings Rhodes's share was six wickets for 27. Something 'always happens' in a Roses match, and in the first of these Yorkshire wrought even greater havoc upon Lancashire than they had upon M.C.C. With a total of under 150 they secured another innings victory. Through the season Rhodes pressed relentlessly on: once more his normal bag from an innings was five, six or seven wickets, and even, as at Catford against Kent, eight. His figures for the match were twelve for 52. Yorkshire lost only one match in the season and that, by some odd inevitability, was against Somerset, but in almost every other game Rhodes completely dominated the situation. Middlesex, Warwickshire, Essex, Gloucestershire, and M.C.C. (as visitors to Scarborough) all felt the full weight of his attack. In these three seasons of almost unchallenged triumph Yorkshire had great strength in batting and fielding, but the solid foundation of their greatness lay in their bowling, and the cornerstone of that foundation was Wilfred Rhodes.

III

In Yorkshire's opening game of 1903, played as usual against M.C.C. at Lord's, a coming event cast a substantial shadow before. Rhodes was asked to go in first. This task he undertook with his own brand of serious concentration and batted with such resolution that he carried his bat through the innings for 98. Only the human fallibility of Yorkshire's

No. 11 robbed him of his maiden century. After this incursion into the higher ranks of batting he returned modestly to the position of No. 6 and resumed concentration on bowling. In a game against Worcestershire early in the season he accomplished the marathon labour of bowling ninety overs in the match, taking in all fourteen wickets for 211. This punishment heavily tired him, as well it might, and for the three weeks that followed—the longest dark patch in his career—he could do scarcely anything right. There appeared in the score-book a none for 101 against Middlesex and a two for 135 against Sussex, and it seemed that Rhodes was set for his first poor season.

But three dark weeks were not to make a black summer. Back to form he came, helping to dismiss Notts for a mere song, his share being seven wickets for 40. Then, after a highly combative innings of 79 against Leicestershire he pulled out from his sleeve his most fantastic trick of the season. On the county ground at Huddersfield—almost, you might say, on his home pitch—he took five Worcestershire wickets for 4 runs and in the second innings was forced to stop at a mere three for 8 because at this stage there were no more victims left. From that moment he proceeded to march through the season like a conquering invader. Henceforth there was scarcely a game in which he did not either score 50 runs or take five wickets in an innings. Sometimes he would do both. Occasionally he would take five wickets in each innings, and one tremendous match took place at the Oval in which Hirst and Rhodes bowled right through the game without a change and shared the wickets equally between them.

And then there was another battle of giants. It was fought at Bradford and dedicated to John Tunnicliffe's benefit. Lancashire were the enemy and they disputed the issue every inch of the way. But they fought in vain against the cunning of Rhodes; in the first innings he was content with five wickets, but in the second, in his elegant, deliberate way, he practically ran amok. On the second evening Hirst bowled MacLaren and, on the third morning, F. S. Jackson bowled Jack Sharp. Rhodes attended with dispatch to all the rest. Eight for 61 was his figure and, to give the story a happy ending, he and Hirst came together when Yorkshire had lost five wickets. With 50 runs still needed against a hostile attack which included Sydney Barnes, the White Rose had appeared to be in danger of wilting. The moment Rhodes joined Hirst, the picture changed and resistance stiffened. Within an hour, and with Barnes still bowling like a demon, the two lads from Kirkheaton had hit off the runs and Yorkshire had won by five wickets.

CHAPTER THIRTEEN

Sticky Dog Down Under

'Just once, Wilf, won't you give us a minute's peace?'
—Victor Trumper

I

The M.C.C. team that toured Australia under P. F. Warner in 1903-4 was reckoned by sophisticated persons to be one of the weakest ever to leave England's shore, and it was freely stated that a far stronger side could have been put together from among those gentlemen of England who, for some reason or another, sat at home at ease. Now sophistication is like money. Few people have it and those few often have too much. In this instance the sophisticated critics were wrong and the team's more simple-minded supporters were right. Warner's men came back with results which confounded alike their foes and their candid friends. There were batting triumphs by R. E. Foster, most brilliant of a formidable brotherhood, and at least one be-wildering exploit by B. J. T. Bosanquet, only begetter of the googly, or 'bosie'; and there were two Test matches, the first at Sydney and the second at Melbourne, which were as dramatic as even the historic encounters of 1902.

Yet, in a broad sense, the most potent factor in the success of the tour was Wilfred Rhodes. His early exploits should have sounded a warning in Australian ears. With no particular help from the wicket he set his mark on the early State matches by taking five for 26 against Victoria and six for 55 against New South Wales. The first Test was, in my opinion, a classic model of what all Tests should be. If I wanted to write a vivid novel with a picturesque Test match background, I should be inclined to lift the characters and episodes from this game *en bloc*, just altering the names here and there, and who would be the hero, R. E. Foster, Trumper or Rhodes, I should not like to say.

Warner lost the toss on a pitch that was a batsman's paradise, and his men might well have resigned themselves to a bowler's purgatory, but the Australians started wretchedly, their first three wickets went down like ninepins, and only a stubborn captain's 100 by Noble brought them along to the respectable total of 287. England started almost as sadly, but then occurred that miracle of batsmanship which flowed from the wand of R. E. Foster, whose score of 287 remained a Test record till Bradman, and an England record till Hutton. Nor was Foster's feat a monumental edifice built slowly brick by brick. After a necessarily circumspect start, his batting blossomed into one of the most dazzling displays of late cutting and off-driving ever seen by a cricket crowd. He received sterling help from Braund, but then the batting unaccountably wavered and, though Foster continued to scintillate, England were only lifted back to the heights by the fighting efforts of the last two wickets. Albert Relf built up a useful 31 and then No. 11 walked briskly to the wicket, as he had walked to the middle at the Oval eighteen months before. By the time he left the crease he had scored 40 not out by flawless batting and had honourably taken part in the record Test match stand for the last wicket. Rhodes had helped Foster to raise the score to 577, and this was another record total for Test matches until Bradman arose and virtually commanded: 'There shall be no more records!'

But this fantastic game had only begun. Australia were in the red to the alarming extent of nearly 300 runs, and yet their recovery was complete. This was due to the collective courage of the side and to the individual splendour of Victor Trumper. The number of candidates for the honour of having played the noblest and most beautiful innings ever played by mortal man is necessarily small: Ranji, Jessop, Macartney, Bradman, and one or two, but only one or two, more, might be named in a very short list. Trumper's score of 185 not out was even more dazzling than R. E. Foster's 287. It was glory, it was wonder. Old men who saw it recall it with tears, and Australians are not easily moved to tears (too right they are not). It was said that Trumper had three strokes for every ball. That day he had five, and no spectator at Sydney Oval ever doubted to the end of his days that, whatever had been and whatever might come, Trumper had made life worth while.

But there was another Richmond in the field, less spectacular but no less heroic. On that heart-breaking pitch, unresponsive as a crystal ice-rink, while Trumper's bat flashed like the brand Excalibur, making lightnings in the splendour of the sun, Rhodes bowled all day, remorseless, relentless, never relaxing length or direction for one instant. One after another he sent them down, forty mortal overs compounded of toil and sweat, if not blood and tears. Of the torrent of runs that flowed that day, less than one fifth came from his bowling, and he took half the wickets that fell. Toward the end of the day Trumper spoke to Rhodes and all his nature, all his gaiety and charm were in the question.

'Wilf,' he implored with humorous exasperation, 'just once, won't you give me a bit of peace?'

And all Rhodes's nature was in the answer.

'No,' he replied. (Or, as we say in Yorkshire, 'Na—w.')

Then he sent down a superlative maiden over, each ball of which would have bowled any batsman but Trumper.

Fifty-four years later I recalled this magnificent 'bit' of bowling to him. 'You took five for 93,' I said, a little complacent about my good memory.

'Na—w,' said Rhodes with the air of a man who will take no more than his due, 'it was five for 94.'

II

At Melbourne in the second Test match he performed what was not necessarily his best, but was by far his most important bowling feat; it was, indeed, the most sensational exploit in England *v.* Australia matches before Verity (1934) and Laker (1956). Let it be granted that the wicket was sufficiently evil to be just what Rhodes might have prayed for and that England had made a solid score before it had worsened. Nevertheless, he bowled as no English or Australian bowler of his time could have bowled and, despite two further deeds of heroism from Trumper, he took seven for 56 and eight for 68. The Melbourne crowds barracked him with a kind of amiable irritation. There was nothing in his rhythmic movement and graceful swing that they could criticize and so they chanted in time with his easy steps to the crease: 'One, two, three, *plunk*; one, two three, *plunk* . . .' Rhodes bowled on, completely imperturbable. There was an epidemic of missed chances or the scores would have been smaller. Nobody knows the cause of the epidemic, though, in Tom Emmett's hallowed phrase, it 'wasn't catching'. Hirst told me, searching his memory with some amusement: 'I was the only man who didn't miss one, but that was only because one never came my way.'

My own belief, supported by no authority, is that the ball had become excessively greasy from contact with the wet (but drying) ground and that every time it left the edge of the bat—that is, from everybody's bat but Trumper's—it went spinning away with the utmost viciousness. At least eight catches were dropped off Rhodes, and yet he took fifteen wickets. Apart from two Ajax-like defiances by Trumper, Australia's batsmen were completely demoralized and Rhodes was the sole architect of their ruin.

Another devastating deed was done a month later on the same sort of pitch on the same ground in the State match against Victoria. On the first day the home side put together

269 for four on an easy wicket; twenty-four hours of semi-tropical rain intervened and then Rhodes polished off the rest of the innings, taking five wickets for practically nothing and bringing his figures to six for 62. England batted on an equally nasty pitch but, mainly owing to courageous work by Warner and Hayward, struggled along until they were only fifty runs behind. It was then that Rhodes, and to a lesser degree Arnold, started out on a policy of virtual annihilation. Victoria were all out in three-quarters of an hour for 15. The wicket was atrocious, but no worse than the one on which England had made 248. One batsman was absent ill, but as he was No. 11 and had made none in the first innings, I cannot feel that his presence would have made a massive difference. The two English bowlers shared the nine wickets, but Rhodes's bag was heavier:

	Overs	Mdns	Runs	Wkts
Arnold . .	6	2	8	4
Rhodes . .	6.1	3	6	5

It is a pity that all the adjectives indicating surprise are called upon too often. The words 'astonishing,' 'astounding', and 'amazing' would for once have been justified.

England lost the third and fifth Tests, and in the latter game Hugh Trumble exacted revenge for what Rhodes had done, to the tune of seven wickets for 28 runs. But England won the fourth game and with it the rubber. This was Bosanquet's match and the failure of the Australians in their second innings to cope with his bewildering googly was a major cause of defeat, but Rhodes bowled remarkably well in their first innings, gaining four wickets for 33. He also batted boldly on a wicket he would have preferred to bowl on, helping his captain to add a valuable 55 for England's last wicket. But Australian spectators could hardly know as yet how much they were to see of his batting in years to come.

CHAPTER FOURTEEN

Time of Transition

'The story of Wilfred Rhodes told as a schoolboy romance would stretch credulity to breaking point.'—J. M. Kilburn

I

THE HOME season following a tiring tour is rarely an outstanding one for any player, and what might have been reckoned an excellent season for another cricketer was only a moderate one for Wilfred Rhodes. True, he once more scored his 1,000 runs and took his 100 wickets, confirming what was to become a settled habit. There was a steady run of creditable bowling performances, if few spectacular ones, for a man cannot take 131 wickets in a season without being fairly consistent. Against Essex and Hampshire he took ten wickets in each game and against Warwickshire at Edgbaston he demonstrated his independence of the state of the wicket, for there he took six for 95 on a batsman's pitch and six for 27 on a bowler's.

In batting he had the most fruitful season of his career so far, although most of the time he filled the modest position of No. 6 or No. 7. So accomplished a player at No. 7 tended to carry out his bat and his early scores included one or two eighties and nineties not out. In the second innings of the first Surrey match he hit up 107 in near-Jessopian style at more than a run a minute, driving, as a normally sober critic said, 'in truly superb style'. In the away game against Worcestershire he amassed—that is the right word—the highest total he had yet made. This was 196, and for some odd reason the description of the game in *Wisden* failed to mention it. (Perhaps the writer still wished to discourage a heaven-sent bowler from descending to the lower status of excellent batsman.) In two later games Rhodes went in first, though without causing any sensations, but when he returned to the post of No. 7, he scored 76 against Middlesex, who by means of Bosanquet's googlies had twice had York-shire in trouble. (Yorkshire, to do them justice, twice fought their way out of the trouble, once thanks to Rhodes and then thanks to Hirst.) After the Middlesex match Rhodes finished the season with a gay array of bowling feats which must have been a warning reassurance to those who were afraid he was batting too well.

II

The year 1905 was F. S. Jackson's year, England's year, and (rather unexpectedly) Yorkshire's year. England, under Jackson's vigorous captaincy, soundly defeated the visiting Australians, and Yorkshire, although robbed of some of their leading players by the Tests, carried off the county champion-ship. As for Rhodes, it seemed almost impossible for him to to go on to a field without achieving some extraordinary exploit with bat or ball, or with both. In the first county game, against Somerset at Taunton, he compiled what was to be the second highest score of his career; in his 201 he hit a six and 31 fours and he built up the massive total with an unruffled determination that must have recalled W. G. Grace. And he did this from the comparatively humble position of No. 7.

On the same south-west tour he took five Gloucestershire wickets for 36 and six Worcestershire wickets for 87; and right through the season he was bringing off bowling feats which confounded his critics. Perhaps six for 16 against Cambridge University was in the nature of taking candy from a child, and it may be that the Essex batsmen of that season were not reaching their best form when, at Hudders-field, Rhodes dismissed six men in their second innings for 9.

On the other hand, the Notts batsmen were not guileless children; yet in the second innings of the game at Sheffield Rhodes and Haigh got rid of the whole side for 39. Rhodes's share was four wickets for 15; and in the return match he took five for 34. Trent Bridge was becoming a favourite ground for his depredations.

Sometimes there were games when he both batted and bowled with supreme skill; and this was almost invariably drawn out in the hardest games. In the tremendous cut-and-thrust Bank Holiday Roses match he overrode the Lancashire batsmen with five wickets for 66 and four for 49, and when Yorkshire's second-innings batting faltered he rallied the ranks with an attacking 74, which played a vital part in Yorkshire's 44-runs victory. The next game, played against Surrey, saw him bring out a similar all-round effort, for he took six wickets in the first innings and four, at small cost, in the second; his innings of 59 not out once more screwed his fellow-batsmen's determination to the sticking-point and substantially helped Yorkshire to win.

In representative matches, where a place was now found for him as a matter of course, he had an interesting, if un-exciting, season. In Tests against Australia his work could hardly be called characteristic. That is, in the first he played two valuable knocks of 29 and 39 not out, but Jackson and Bosanquet took the labours and honours of the bowling off his hands. In the fourth Test he scored 27 not out and took two for 25 and three for 36. My Uncle Walter, who watched this game, told me that Rhodes would have taken several more wickets if only his captain had put him on sooner. Mr Jackson, Uncle Walter maintained, should have known better.

Two other big games redounded to Rhodes's credit. In the Gentlemen v. Players match at the Lord's he took three for 48 and five for 71, enjoying the heightened pleasure of counting Jackson and Jessop among his victims. And to finish off a fine bowling season, he took eleven wickets in the Champion County *v.* the Rest game. He was not yet the leading all-rounder in the country, but his stride was lengthening.

III

Without question 1906, as we have seen, was to be marked in the calendar as Hirst's year. Nobody has ever equalled his record of 2,000 runs and 200 wickets, and nobody, in my judgement, ever will. An effort which came within challenging distance was that achieved by Rhodes the year before. To score 1,581 runs and take 182 wickets is to prove yourself an all-rounder of the highest quality, well worth your place in a representative side for either batting or bowling. It was only the third time that this remarkably gifted technician had reached his 1,000 runs and 100 wickets: doubles galore were still to come. Yet in this season of 1906 when he made 1,721 runs and took 128 wickets, his critics were particularly severe on him. They remained unimpressed by his frequent scores of 70, 80, and 90, not to mention a trio of centuries; they were not even appeased when he took five wickets for 40 against Warwickshire or five for 49 in one more fiercely contested Roses match at Old Trafford. Nothing could excuse his declension, and the worst aspect of it was that he had now begun, with some regularity, to go in first. 'The fact remains', said *Wisden*, 'that his continued advance as a batsman did not compensate for his marked decline as a bowler. . . . He had lost his quick spin off the pitch and, on hard wickets, batsmen did not fear him in the least. Even his delivery was not quite the same. . . . Rhodes is still such a young man that the distinctive qualities of his bowling may come back to him, but for the moment he must be regarded as an all-round cricketer. It would have been better for Yorkshire if he had remained a specialist, made fewer runs, and still remained a great bowler.'

'Poor old Sydney Pardon,' chuckled Rhodes to me at Bournemouth. 'He never would pardon me.'

It would be easy for hind-sight to re-edit the passage from *Wisden* with slightly uproarious exclamation marks, but, to be fair to a genius's critics, they could not know that the greatest bowler in the world was genuinely capable of becoming the second greatest batsman of his period and then of becoming once more over several seasons the leading bowler in the country. It shows that the way of the critic is hard.

Incidentally, this was the year when Yorkshire lost the championship, and lost it, to their exasperation, by a single run. In the last match but one, against Gloucestershire at Bristol, they were set 234 runs to get to win, and when Ringrose, the last man, went in, eleven of these were still needed. Now Ringrose, though a fast bowler of merit, had a batting average of 3·00. Hubert Myers, holding the fort with courage at the other end, resourcefully protected him from peril, scoring 9 precious runs as he did so. But the luckless Ringrose, like the luckless Tate at Old Trafford in 1902, was forced by fate to face the music at last. Jessop, Gloucestershire's captain, took the ball himself and very nearly settled the matter out of hand by bowling down the leg-side a fast near-wide which, but for a wild goal-keeper's leap by Jack Board, might have gone for four byes and a Yorkshire victory. The next ball hit Ringrose hard on the pad and, after a wild appeal and an authentic breathless hush, the umpire raised his finger. That finger raised Kent into the first place in the championship.

In Yorkshire they took it 'hard' and their sense of having been robbed by a malign fate was deep and strong. After the season, the Yorkshire cricketers paid their annual visit at their captain's invitation to his country home at Wighill Park, and it was impossible wholly to exclude discussion of the team's unhappy one-run defeat. So on St Helena

Napoleon never for long ceased wondering what exactly had gone wrong at Waterloo. It was hard to avoid the subject. Over the tea-cups Lord Hawke's sister was heard to murmur to the tallish, good-looking young man sitting next to her: 'Now I wonder who was the wretched man who got out when only two runs were needed.'

The tallish, good-looking young man blushed like a beetroot. 'It was me, ma'am,' confessed Mr Ringrose.

Now what should a kind lady, who never meant to hurt anyone's feelings in her life, have said then?

IV

In the wet season of 1907 Rhodes regained some lost favour by 'going back' to bowling. Those who had previously reproved him recognized the change and admitted, rather astonishingly, that he had made up the ground he had lost the year before and that in many matches he had been something like himself. What the critics had continually in mind was, of course, the magical year of 1900, when Rhodes took 261 wickets, still the highest number ever obtained by a Yorkshire bowler. To the people who with awe-stricken arithmetic counted up Rhodes's wickets between 1898 and 1903—the fantastic figures totalled 1,251—any fall from such heights must have seemed disastrous. Any dangerous deviation into good batting must have appeared fraught with peril. When, in 1907, his batting average fell from 30 to 23, there were scattered cheers. 'Making fewer runs,' said *Wisden,* 'he naturally came fresher to his more important work.'

Certainly he started off on the West Country tour with which the county started their season as if he meant to excel in bowling and in nothing else. Six for 61 and six for 69 against Somerset; five for 72 against Gloucestershire; and four for 78 and five for 58 against Worcestershire—these happy figures seemed to be an earnest of the way he meant to go on. In the Whitsuntide game against Lancashire, after a day had been completely lost through rain, Rhodes brought Yorkshire's batting back to respectability by scoring 68 at a time when his side looked as though they might have to follow on; then, when Lancashire went in again, he bowled with a craft that brought him six for 46.

There was hardly a game, as the season progressed, when he did not capture five or six wickets in an innings, and no county could treat his bowling with disrespect. So far that year he had batted in no higher position than No. 7, but in the game against Sussex at Bramall Lane he was tried once more at No. 1. The death of J. T. Brown had severed the strongest first-wicket partnership that Yorkshire had had so far, and the impending retirement of Tunnicliffe revealed another gap. Rhodes was only one of the batsmen tried for the post, but his merit was obvious, for he brought to batting the same qualities that had always informed his bowling: steadiness, consistency, unhurried concentration.

His 112 against Leicestershire was a model of what an innings by a reliable opening bat ought to be, but after a few games he ceded the opening position to Rothery, a stylish young batsman from Harrogate, who, for a time at least, held the post with credit. Rhodes's bowling did not suffer from his temporary promotion. Against Derbyshire at Glossop he and Hirst bowled unchanged throughout the match, getting rid of their opponents twice for a little over 100 in all. Virtually the same thing happened in the return game with Leicestershire at Hull, though it was Hirst who took the lion's share of the spoils. In the Roses match at Headingley Rhodes so dominated the game with ball and bat that he took six wickets in the first innings and five in the second. Then, batting again at No. 6, because F. S. Jackson was playing his one game of the season, he restored Yorkshire's morale when they were in danger of stumbling. His 69 was the highest score in the game, and his batting, bowling, and fielding combined to make him the man of the

Yorkshire Post

'*I never hope to see a better coach or a better man*'—Bill Bowes

GEORGE HIRST AT 75

'An old gentleman with a still keen eye and a still brimming love of cricket.'

'*From 1898 to 1903 this miraculous young bowler
took 1,251 wickets.*'

YORKSHIRE CAP AND ENGLAND BLAZER

victorious match. At Canterbury he helped Hirst to drag
the game out of jeopardy (Rhodes, 95; Hirst, 91 not out)
and Kent, after being well on top of their opponents, were
lucky to escape with a draw.

Rhodes's critics might have argued that his persistence in
doing two things well instead of one thing supremely well
had robbed him of his place in the three Tests against the
South African tourists this soaking summer. Plainly, dependable though he was, he was not yet an opening batsman
to be compared with such masters as C. B. Fry and Tom
Hayward; on the other hand, there was one left-arm slow
bowler who, that year at any rate, surpassed him. This was
Colin Blythe of Kent. There will always be argument
among older judges of the game as to the comparative
merits of Rhodes and Blythe. Both were, of course, in the
very highest flight and Ranjitsinhji once said that Blythe's
'flighting' of the ball was even more deceptive than Rhodes's.
Blythe, a lovable character who was killed in the first
World War, had some wonderful matches and some wonderful seasons, but he did not have Rhodes's physical
strength and consistency and he never bowled quite so well
as did Rhodes in his first five seasons, as often as not on
batsmen's wickets.

In 1907 the seasonal figures of the two bowlers were
almost identical: Blythe, 183 wickets at an average of 15·42,
and Rhodes, 177 at 15·57. But Blythe was picked for the
first Test. Then in the second, at Leeds, on a wicket that
Yorkshire folk believed would have suited Rhodes equally
well, he bowled superbly. His match record of fifteen
wickets for 99 surpassed Rhodes's Melbourne record of
three years before. Blythe was the man of the match, and
indeed the man of the series, and no Yorkshireman could
grudge him his triumph, particularly as his health was never
robust and at Leeds he had bowled literally until he drooped.

But Rhodes went steadfastly on his way.

V

The interlude for Rhodes between the seasons for 1907 and 1908 was his visit to Australia with A. O. Jones's unlucky touring team. On paper they looked, and in one or two State matches they showed themselves to be, a splendid combination, but in Tests they were both unfortunate and singularly ineffective. At No. 7 Rhodes did his duty admirably, helping to stiffen a batting side that showed unexpected and alarming chinks in its armour. In all matches he was third in the batting averages, gaining a place above Hobbs. In his capacity as a change bowler, however, he came well below J. N. Crawford, Fielder, and Barnes. This was, for him, a period of transition. But England was not to be the loser by it.

CHAPTER FIFTEEN

Bowler into Batsman

'Now, Wilfred, no more than twenty.'—Lord Hawke

I

IN 1908 Yorkshire recovered, without a single defeat, the championship which had slipped through their fingers in the two previous seasons. Of all his sides, Lord Hawke reserved an especially soft spot in his heart for his 1908 eleven, if only because the season marked his twenty-fifth year of captaincy. Yorkshire triumphed first and foremost, as always, through the power of their bowling, which was reinforced by a lively newcomer, J. T. Newstead. If you want proof of a championship side's true quality, whether it be the Surrey of today or the Yorkshire of the day before yesterday, look at their season's bowling figures. By this test Yorkshire's 1908 side stands out as one of the strongest of all county elevens.

Their batting too was also of exceptional merit. Denton and Hirst were as dashing as ever; the county's chief difficulty was to find an opening partner for Rhodes, now acknowledged as authentic No. 1 batsman, and the compiler of three excellent centuries during the season. Several young players were tried, including Rothery, Hardisty, and B. B. Wilson, but the ideal collaborator had not yet been discovered. As a matter of fact Rhodes never found quite the partner he wanted in county cricket; his ideal companion was, of course, Jack Hobbs and no other.

Though his batting had grown so powerful, those who had previously frowned on it could hardly complain, because his bowling, even in competition with Hirst, Haigh, and the newcomer, Newstead, was powerful, too. Usually he was put on at the later stage of an innings, if only because the other bowlers were normally so successful; indeed, he bowled some 300 overs less than Hirst and 200 less than Newstead. (Haigh, who for long periods was actually the deadliest of the four, was out of the game for a long time with a broken finger.) Yet Rhodes took his 100 wickets and, though it might be said that his bigger scores were made against some of the lightweight counties, his most penetrating bowling pierced the defences of much stronger opposition. In another pull-devil-pull-baker Roses match at Sheffield he and Hirst polished off Lancashire's second innings in less than an hour on the third morning, and, in a rain-bespattered game against Notts at Headingley the same pair virtually wiped their opponents off the map. In these two innings Rhodes's share of the spoils was four for 30 and six for 33. In the return Roses game he had one of those charming sets of figures which, without being spectacular, give thoughtful pleasure to the bowler:

Overs	Mdns	Runs	Wkts
9	5	11	3

If you can imagine the tenseness of the normal Lancashire v. Yorkshire game, you can see how tightly every one of those overs was bowled. In the game against M.C.C. at Scarborough Rhodes needed five wickets to complete his 100 in county matches. (This was a county match, though not, of course, a championship one.) Early in M.C.C.'s innings he captured his first by forcing the immaculate Spooner to make a false stroke; for some time after that the batsmen resisted obstinately, and it seemed that with ninety-six his limit had been reached. Then, late in the afternoon, Lord Hawke tossed him the ball for the third time and almost at once he ran through the rest of the side, taking four for 9. Even the worst of his best friends must have admitted that this was not ineffective for a No. 1 batsman.

II

The year 1909 saw England beaten by Australia in the second successive rubber and there was a general feeling among usually reasonable people that this defeat should not have happened. In normal circumstances it is both absurd and unfair to rail against selectors as a body. At least they want to pick a winning team as much as do their critics and they must be presumed to know a little more about the general situation. Nevertheless, the England selectors of 1909 appear to stand convicted of an incursion into the larger lunacy. In short, they picked too many players and then left the wrong ones out, so that in the end twenty-six players were tried. Thus, many were called, but only eleven at a time could be chosen. The sorrows of the selectors became pathetic. England won the first game, but that was the end of their fun. After that they lost two games and had by far the worst of two draws. For the second Test Jessop was unaccountably left out, and Brearley, who lacked the meekness of Moses, anticipated his own dropping by dropping himself first. After that, virtually every player found himself in the side in one match and out of it in the next, and only the captain and the wicket-keeper played in all five. The greatest tragedy of all was that Jessop, brought back into the side for the third game, was cruelly injured during the first hour's fielding, and played no more, not only in that game, but all the rest of that season.

Rhodes played in four matches and acquitted himself meritoriously; that is, he had a higher batting record than Hobbs, though a slightly inferior one to Lilley, the wicket-keeper, who, after all, was four times not out. By the time the fifth Test had been reached, Rhodes had been promoted to No. 3 and in that position he scored 66 and 54. He was not often called on to bowl, but when this happened, as in Australia's first innings at Leeds, he again performed with credit; his four for 38 was the best 'bit of bowling' that

England produced during the series. In the drawn game at Old Trafford, when the Australians in their second innings were hitting the English attack all over the place, Barnes and Blythe, those splendid bowlers, temporarily lost their grip on the game. It was then that Rhodes bowled like an angel. He received some cavalier handling from the dazzlingly aggressive bat, Macartney, but he bowled him in the end, and his five wickets on that day of dolour for bowlers cost him only 16 runs apiece. This Test series, unhappy though its outcome was for England, showed Rhodes as undoubtedly the most reliable all-rounder in the side. At the same time, it marked the first occasion on which he was picked for his country as a batsman rather than as a bowler.

By now his eccentricity in being a more valuable batsman than a bowler was nearly forgiven. 'He has now become such an exceptionally good batsman,' said *Wisden*, 'that the regret one used to feel at his ever giving his mind to run-getting has lost its force.'

This was nicely said. To make over 2,000 runs, including five centuries, is to be a good batsman by any standard, and if, on top of that, you take more than 140 wickets, then, I think, you may reasonably suggest that the critics hold their peace. Rhodes never went long without doing something of note, whether it was scoring 199 and 84 against Sussex on the run-rich ground at Hove or taking six wickets for 36 against Middlesex on a rain-soaked pitch at Lord's. Nor, in scoring his centuries and taking six wickets in an innings at least a dozen times, did he ever forget that, first and foremost, he belonged to a fighting county. Certain matches were more like pitched battles than games, and these, in his undemonstrative way, he enjoyed most of all. I remember once asking him to describe the atmosphere of a Roses battle.

'Oh, well,' he said, 'the Lancashire chaps were a bit keen, but', he added with a perfectly straight face, 'we didn't bother all that much. . . .'

It was in this spirit that he took seven for 68 and six for 40 to defeat Lancashire in Schofield Haigh's benefit match. His most combative effort of the season was his effort to stave off defeat at Huddersfield in the game against Kent which Yorkshire lost after having been forced to follow on 250 runs behind. In their second innings Rhodes and Hirst came together in the most heroic stand of the match, and so long as either of them was still in there was always a chance that the game could be saved. Of all the hundreds that he scored during the season, that 101, every run of which was fought for in a plainly losing game, was the most courageous; his 101 against a strong M.C.C. side at Scarborough was the most carefree; and his 108 for Yorkshire against the Australians was the most solid and rewarding, for it laid the foundations of his next, and most triumphant, encounter with Australia in 1911-12.

III

He had already had two tours of Australia, one as a bowler and one as an all-rounder. The English winter of 1910-11 saw him travelling to South Africa under P. F. Warner's captaincy. England lost the rubber by two games to three, and somewhere down the order there was weakness in the England batting, which, it might be said, consisted of Hobbs, Denton, and Rhodes, with the rest of the side virtually nowhere. Rhodes made 66 in the first Test match and 44 in the second, in each case coming second top-scorer to Hobbs. In the Third Test Rhodes did little; the game, which England won by three wickets, belonged to David Denton, who scored his third dashing 100 in successive innings, and to Hobbs, who, without any heroics, rose from a sick bed to make 93 not out. Then, after failing completely in the fourth Test, Rhodes in the fifth shared with Hobbs a glorious first-wicket partnership of 221, which set England well on the road to a nine-wicket win. This smooth-running, happy partnership delighted all who witnessed it, except, perhaps, the South African fielders. It indicated the shape of things to come, for England a most valuable shape indeed.

IV

After the Lord Mayor's Show traditionally comes the dust-cart, and after a dozen seasons at, or near, the head of the county table Yorkshire fell to eighth place, just above Northamptonshire. This, in such peaceful times, seemed the end of the world, at least for Yorkshire people, and there was a good deal of breast-beating around the Ridings. A little philosophy in such affairs has been learnt since then and the opinion was even put forward at the time that 'in cricket, as in more important matters, a change of fortune is most acutely felt by those who have enjoyed great prosperity'. The change of fortune, falling heavily on the county, affected the players in various ways. Trouble was meat and drink to Hirst, who, as we have already seen, had one of his grandest seasons. Rhodes, on paper at least, had one of his poorest. But a poor season for Rhodes is like a poor play by Shakespeare: only poor for him. For the first time in eight successive seasons he broke his sequence of doubles, yet to score 1,465 runs and take 88 wickets is a more than reputable achievement. What must be remembered is that Rhodes had now become second- or even third-change bowler in Yorkshire's varied attack, and then it was his business, not to dismiss tail-enders cheaply, but more often than not to break some troublesome stand. The clearest example of this custom occurred in the second innings of the Derbyshire game at Bradford. When Rhodes began to bowl, Derbyshire, on an admittedly horrid wicket, had reached 50 for four; eight overs later, they were all out and his record ran:

Overs	Mdns	Runs	Wkts
4.4	2	5	5

It was a triumph of perfect length and remorseless exploitation of the batsmen's difficulties.

On the same ground, where the pitch had so often helped him, he experienced his most heartening game of the season. In a low-scoring game against Surrey, he played the hero with bat and ball. In two devastating bowling spells he took five wickets for 38 and then six for 38. The kind of wicket that had delighted him as a bowler could delight nobody as a batsman. Yet when Yorkshire were set 157 to win, a daunting task on such a mud-heap, so determined was his batting in both attack and defence that he mastered the bothersome bowling of Razor Smith and brought Yorkshire along to victory by five wickets almost single-handed. Apart from himself only one person reached double figures. Only a player of the calibre of W.G. himself could have truly relished a game of that kind.

V

The Yorkshire club gratefully gave Rhodes a benefit in 1911, an honour which normally marks the autumn of a good and faithful servant. How were they to know that he was not yet half-way through his first-class cricketing life? It was a fine summer, as dry and warm as 1910 had been wet and miserable. Once more he scored over 2,000 runs, not a difficult achievement for an accomplished batsman in a batsman's year; but he also took 117 wickets and that kind of double is exceedingly rare. That Yorkshire in such a year should have fallen from championship grace was assuredly not the fault of their chief all-rounder.

In 1911 Yorkshire came seventh in the table, and though they won in fact more victories than Warwickshire, the deservedly popular champions, they lost as many as eight games, and this was a most un-Yorkshirelike fate. Rhodes just ran past Hirst in batting and Hirst had better figures in bowling, but they were both still immensely formidable all-rounders. While either of them was in form serious losses were unlikely to occur. The county's weaknesses sprang from other sources. Rhodes's first high score (exactly 100) was made against Derbyshire at Sheffield in Yorkshire's first game at home: his last two comprised a couple of hundreds (128 and 115) against M.C.C. in the relaxed but bracing air of the Scarborough Festival. This scoring of two separate centuries in a single game was one of the few record-books feats that Rhodes had not yet accomplished. One feels that he ticked it off with his usual accuracy.

In between, there was a masterly 125 against Sussex at Leeds and a splendid 121 in the England *v.* the Rest Test Trial at Lord's, though it seems absurd to suggest that Rhodes needed a Test Trial. The tale of his five hundreds does not register the extent of his full value, for he made as many nineties, including 95 against Kent and 91 against Surrey in a game where Yorkshire, by an obstinate rearguard action, fought their way out of defeat.

In bowling he pursued his calm, methodical way: on batsman's wickets he bore the burden and endured some punishment, as when, for instance, he sent down 43 overs against Essex, with a reward of only two wickets for 124. Whoever thinks that he bowled feebly on that occasion does not know his Rhodes. On the other hand, if things 'went his way', he was relentless. With a cruel sun shining on a damaged wicket at Chesterfield, he went on at a point when Derbyshire, struggling gamely, had scored 65 for one; when he had finished with his victims they were all out for the meagre addition of 46 runs and he had taken seven for 16.

Not always did his valuable efforts bring the success they merited. Weak first-innings batting (not Rhodes's) allowed Yorkshire to be beaten by Surrey, in spite of Rhodes's capture of six wickets for 29. And in what turned out to be their hardest contest of the season, against an exceedingly aggressive Northamptonshire, Rhodes took fourteen wickets

in all, but Yorkshire, mainly through a display of bad fielding
that was as rare as it was reprehensible, lost the game by
44 runs.

In his benefit match against the old enemy he had to
struggle for his wickets, because Lancashire, after having
been over 100 behind, scored heavily in their second innings
and Rhodes in his 31 overs suffered a savage belabouring
from K. G. McLeod, who batted exactly like the splendid
Rugby footballer he was. Rhodes's figures that day of four
for 109 represent the work of a man who has passed through
the great tribulation, but passed with honours. For some
unexplained reason the gate at this match was comparatively
small, much too small for a tribute to the man to whom
Yorkshire and English cricket owed so much. The county
authorities therefore launched a special reminder, and as
subscriptions rolled in they were able to announce that the
beneficiary would receive £2,200. This was a seemingly
modest sum in comparison with the literally inflated benefits
of the present day, but a snug nest-egg in the pre-1914
period. Every pound of those 2,200 was worth a pound, and
no less. By the time the final sum was computed Rhodes was
on his way to Australia with the team captained by P. F.
Warner, who had led the last successful tour in 1903-4.

VI

The M.C.C.'s 1911-12 tour of Australia, which started
almost tragically with the severe illness of the English captain, became in the end one of the most triumphant in
touring history. Four Test matches were won and, despite
the absence of a popular captain, who made a fine century
in his first match and then spent most of the rest of the tour
in a nursing home, the team worked splendidly together
under J. W. H. T. Douglas, who may have lacked Warner's
personal charm, but carried with him everywhere a determination to conquer that won the respect of friend and foe.

Coming to more easily assessable matters, there were two main causes for success. The first was the bowling of Barnes and F. R. Foster (who had, so to speak, just stepped on to the boat from leading his county to their first championship). The second was the batting of Hobbs and Rhodes: of Hobbs, the supreme artist, and of Rhodes, the impeccable craftsman. With Rhodes Hobbs founded for England's glory that wonderful Surrey-Yorkshire partnership which at a later date and for a longer period he continued with Herbert Sutcliffe. The polished and (to fieldsmen) bewildering art of swift, sure running between the wickets which was perfected by Hobbs and Sutcliffe was initiated by Hobbs and Rhodes. In this matter Sutcliffe has had no more than his due, but Rhodes has had less. In this 1911-12 tour the running of Hobbs and Rhodes provoked Australian fielders, men not easily rattled, into wild exasperation. To the spectator it usually seemed so sure and so easy; occasionally it looked alarmingly risky, but this was when it was extremely safe. When asked to reveal the secret of this happy and fruitful collaboration, Rhodes would assume a solemn, confidential air. 'I'll tell you,' he would murmur in what D. R. Jardine used to call his 'strangulated voice': 'When I'm coming, I say *Yes*, and when I'm not, I say *No*.'

The answer lay, as it lies with all successful partnerships in other, and perhaps more important, fields than cricket, in perfect understanding and sound judgement. Never did two batsmen develop a more smoothly-working agreement; never did two partners show such superb individual judgement. Those who have seen England players as good as Edrich and as great as Compton floundering in the middle of the pitch like old ladies who have just missed the Women's Institute annual outing bus may perhaps bear with the reminder that Hobbs and Rhodes, not to mention Hobbs and Sutcliffe, could time a short run, without either hesitation or haste, to a fraction of a foot and a fraction of a second. They were run-stealers indeed, but they did not flicker to and fro. Flickering is the exact antithesis of their gleaming certitude. Moreover, when Hobbs said: 'You can always trust Wilfred,' he was not merely thinking of Rhodes's vigilance in batting and intelligence in running, but of his complete integrity as a man.

Rhodes started off with the sort of supremely competent batting that he was to display right through this victorious tour: he made 66 and 64 not out in the State games against Victoria and Queensland; he did nothing much (41 and 0) in the first Test match, which England lost; in the second he scored 61 and 28 and in the third 59 and 57 not out. We will not make too much of his century against Tasmania; after all, Woolley scored 305 not out in the same game; his grandest exploit was his share in England's resounding, rubber-winning victory in the fourth Test. Bowling honours went, as they had almost invariably done, to Foster, Barnes, and Douglas. England's opening pair, Hobbs and Rhodes, scored 323 for the first wicket, an England Test record which was to remain intact until it was broken by Hutton and Washbrook in South Africa thirty-five years later. (Hutton's most slavish admirer asks to be forgiven for thinking that Hobbs and Rhodes faced a more formidable opposition.) Hobbs made 178 and Rhodes one run more, so that in their departure they were scarcely divided. Hobbs's innings was the more dazzling spectacle; Rhodes's was the rock on which the Australian attack broke in vain. In this game Rhodes used an especially heavy bat, lent him by George Gunn, and it stood him in such good stead that many of his firm, perfectly-middled defensive strokes went speeding to the boundary.

The normal characteristic of Rhodes's batting was its sober consistency. It was not often that he ran riot with a bat in his hand. Bowling was a different matter: he had had his orgies of destruction with the ball and, though no one yet knew it, was to have them again. In the great Hobbs-Rhodes combination, he was the solid, though not stolid, partner. But in the return State match against New South Wales he suddenly blossomed forth into what must have been the most exhilarating onslaught of his career. In the first innings he scored 119 in flawless style; in the second, he threw all his Yorkshire caution to the winds and for once batted not so much with his usual disciplined efficiency as with a kind of inspired brilliance which his admirers had never witnessed before. An old Sydney friend of mine who saw this game as a youth told me long afterwards: 'You never saw anything like Wilfred's batting; his first innings was like Hobbs and then, blow me down, if his second wasn't like Trumper.'

This was a memorable saying, because, for a pre-Bradman Australian to bracket a man with Victor Trumper was the highest praise that could be bestowed on any of God's creatures. For those who saw Trumper in the glory of his morning, none could be compared with him but an angel of light.

Praise less extravagant, but equally sincere, was bestowed on Rhodes's fielding.

'He was good anywhere,' said his captain. 'You cannot put him out of place in the field.'

VII

England is not overburdened with bright summers. The season of 1912 was the wettest between Noah and 1958, and because of this, the Triangular Tournament, played between England, Australia, and South Africa, was reckoned a failure. Each side (between showers) played three Tests against the other two and the result was that England came first, Australia second, and South Africa nowhere. It can only be said that if the weather had been less dismal, things might have been better, and that if you are going to invite two sides to tour your country from the other side of the world, then you ought, in all conscience, to provide them with a little more sunshine. Rhodes played for England in all the Tests, and while he did not (nor did anyone else) reach the batting heights of the previous winter's tour he came as before second in the records to Hobbs, and his best scores were 59 in the first Test against Australia; 92 in the second (rain-wrecked) game at Lord's—C. B. Fry said he dug that 92 'out of the slush'—and a valuable 49 in the final vital game at the Oval. It would be idle to claim, however, that England's batting played a vital part in their victories; it was the bowling of Foster, Barnes, and Woolley that did the trick.

Yorkshire won the championship; at any rate the rain allowed them to win thirteen games and lose only one. Rhodes, when not turning out for England, played for Yorkshire his usual completely reliable game. This was a season that saw Denton wielding his bat like D'Artagnan's rapier while Rhodes swung his honest broadsword; or, to put it another way, Rhodes's batting was good ale with roast beef and Yorkshire pudding compared with Denton's champagne and lobster. But what mellow ale, what fine, nourishing roast beef! His contributions were almost always of high value at need, whether it was his 107 in the Whitsuntide Roses match, when nobody else could muster 30, or his heroic 84, which just failed to save the game at Lord's against Middlesex, when the next highest scorer made no more than 22. His most fruitful match was against Notts at Harrogate, where he batted the whole of the first day for 176 and was caught at the wicket off the first ball in the morning. To offset this disappointment he took five wickets for 68 and made sure of Yorkshire victory.

VIII

Yorkshire came second in the county championship in 1913 and reasonably deserved to do well. Rhodes, for that season at least, was their most successful all-rounder, for once out-stripping Hirst in runs and being only a few wickets behind him in bowling. He did not quite reach the standard of his tremendous all-round years, 1909 (2,094 runs and 141 wickets) and 1911 (2,261 runs and 117 wickets), but it was a splendid record for a man whose benefit for substantial service lay two years behind him. His four hundreds, including 152 against Leicestershire, were not made against the strongest opposition, but they were models of the best kind of orthodox batting, including that elegant stroke, the cut, which he afterwards abjured, as not being 'a business stroke'. As had so often happened, too, he came within reach of several more hundreds. He was, almost as much as Woolley, a victim of 'ninetyitis'. There was a solid 97 at Leyton; an 86 not out at Sheffield, with which he carried Yorkshire to a thrilling three-wicket win against Middlesex; and a 90 at the Oval, which was the foundation of a handsome victory over Surrey.

There were few spectacular feats among his steady season's work with the ball, but he took 85 wickets and, in certain important games, he broke the enemy's defences when a break-through was most needed. Particularly deadly was his bowling against Kent at Tunbridge Wells. Here he made the ball bite and turn so swiftly that the five batsmen whom he dismissed at small expense learned, if they had not known it before, that the bowling force named Wilfred Rhodes was far from spent.

IX

For the M.C.C. team that toured South Africa that winter he was an automatic choice. The side was remarkably strong and almost uniformly successful. It was perhaps a pity that the South African cricket of the period was so weak; but even if it had been a great deal stronger this powerful touring side would still have torn it to tatters.

Hobbs and Barnes were the giants, as they had been two years before in Australia, but between Hobbs's splendid batting and Barnes's almost unplayable bowling, there was the solid all-round work of Rhodes, who scored 885 runs and took 57 wickets in all matches. His figures in first-class matches were naturally a little smaller, but his highest score, 152, was made in the second Test match at Johannesburg and laid the foundation of England's innings victory.

He was occasionally barracked by the crowd because he would not hurry to please them, but you cannot hurry a Yorkshireman who knows that initial caution is the best policy for building up an impregnable position. This, incidentally, was the Test in which Sydney Barnes took seventeen wickets—eight for 56 and nine for 103—thus performing the most sensational bowling feat B.L. (before Laker). When the team returned home in triumph they were guests at a centenary dinner at Lord's, at which W.G. made one of his rare speeches. Play, he told them, was getting rather slow—here, I like to think, he solemnly winked at such fellow-guests as Hobbs and Woolley—and what was wanted was to limit Tests to three days. If they couldn't finish in that time, declared the Old Man, let 'em wash the whole thing out and start again.

X

The season of 1914 was history's saddest, though no one knew it at the time. Yorkshire descended to fourth place, and Surrey, becoming leaders for the first time since 1899, assumed the sway that of late years has become near-permanent, richly deserved, and slightly monotonous. Yorkshire were a team of up-and-downers; their best was very good indeed, but when they were bad they were horrid. Rhodes did not bat quite as well as did Hirst and Denton, who had fine, fruitful seasons, but he bowled so destructively that even his most grudging admirers ceased to sigh for the old days. The time when he could take 725 wickets in three seasons was gone for ever, but his 118 in 1914 were well and truly earned, and, combined with 1,377 runs, brought up his tally of doubles to nine. At any rate, if he could still take seven wickets for 19, as he did against Derbyshire at Headingley, Yorkshire followers were content. In their opinion, offered only half-ironically, there was still hope for the lad. But it was in back-to-the-wall games that he showed the fighting quality for which his greatest contemporary was so famous. In the battle royal with Surrey at Bradford which ended in Yorkshire's defeat by 28 runs, he not only scored 89, but took six wickets for 109 and five for 56, figures that show him as a doughty warrior in the thick of the battle. And in the equally exciting game with Middlesex at Bramall Lane, it was his bowling that turned the scale which gave Yorkshire a thrilling two-wicket win.

The season's sun went down in a sinister and gloomy Wagnerian finale. Jack Hobbs's benefit match was removed from the Oval to Lord's. The bust of W.G. was moved from the Long Room for safety, and this, half-solemnly and half-comically, symbolized for cricketers everywhere the end of an innings. The lights, as was nobly and tragically said, were going out all over Europe. Five seasons were to pass before the small, clear light of cricket was to burn again.

CHAPTER SIXTEEN

Back to the Old Love

'The curving line of Rhodes's flight—is there anything in cricket, or in any other game, more lovely to see?'—Neville Cardus

I

WHEN Rhodes returned from the 1911-12 tour of Australia, he attended a dinner given in his honour by one of the many Yorkshire clubs. In a characteristically modest speech in reply to the toast of his health, he thanked the speaker for his compliments and admitted that of late he had had a bit of luck with the bat. 'But,' he added, 'I haven't forgotten about bowling and that's the thing I've always liked best.'

'Nay, Wilfred,' said Arthur Dolphin, the Yorkshire wicket-keeper who was sitting beside him, 'tha never could bowl, anyhow.'

Yorkshire humour is a funny thing. Dolphin's observation, made with the required deadpan face, was of a kind to set the local table in a roar. They laughed because they *knew* Rhodes was a great bowler, however many runs he had been misguided enough to make. Yet not even the most humorous Yorkshireman could realize that after the war Rhodes would start out on a new career as a new bowler.

Without pressing the analogy too far, it may be said that the world of cricket had changed in the same way as had the wider world. Life was real, life was earnest, and the carefree fun of the thing was not its goal. The gay, laughing-cavalier panache of the game dominated by the old amateur was going. The reign of the competent, efficient, businesslike professional was at hand. The comparison, I repeat, must not be exaggerated. Professionals like Hobbs and Woolley possessed the true spirit of the amateur as surely as J. W. H. T. Douglas displayed both the high technical qualities and occupational caution of the typical professional; but, by and large, post-war cricket was no longer for the light of heart.

The change from a pre-war to a typical post-war Roses match was plain for all to see. The difference was as between a dashing cavalry engagement and trench warfare, and now, of course, cavalry were out of date. Before 1914 the majestic line of Lancashire batting advanced with A. C. MacLaren, R. H. Spooner, and Johnny Tyldesley, and Yorkshire's initial charge was led by such cavaliers as Denton, Hirst, and F. S. Jackson. The cricket could not but be gay in such a jocund company. Dourness, at any rate as a major policy, did not appear on either side till after the war. All the stories of 'no fours before lunch and dam' few afterwards' are of post-war vintage. Roy Kilner's dictum, 'We shake hands first morning, and say How do; then we say nowt for three days, but How's that', was current only in the early twenties. Gradually, and with notable exceptions, the dazzlers played out their innings and retired. At Old Trafford Harry Makepeace reigned in their stead. The older glory had departed. And, of course, the most remarkable thing about this metamorphosis is that Wilfred Rhodes moved forward with serene calm from the first period into the second. If there was a gap, he bridged it.

II

To find county cricket opening again, to see white flannels on green turf at Lord's, to hear the noble music of bat on ball—these were among the true joys of peace. There was no apprehension among those returning that cricket might be different; there was only deep pleasure that cricket had come back at all.

During the war, Rhodes, like Hirst and some of his other

fellow-professionals, had done his duty by working during the week on munitions and turning out on Saturday afternoons for one or other of the various north-country league clubs, where the slightly surprised club cricketer might have the honour to be hit for six by Frank Woolley or bowled neck and crop by Sydney Barnes. For at least four years nobody knew when the county championship would start again, if ever. There was even a belief that it might be permanently replaced by League cricket.

The president of a prominent Lancashire League club has told me how in all good faith he came over to Huddersfield to secure Rhodes's signature on a document which would have turned him into a League professional and deprived Yorkshire of his services for ever. Happily the well-meaning kidnapper's quest was in vain, but it was, as the Duke of Wellington said, a near-run thing. I toy with the fancy that the whole of Huddersfield went into mourning that day and that the astonished visitor entered a town of drawn blinds and empty streets. The emotions felt by Yorkshire when Hirst was left out of the Manchester Test in 1902 were experienced once more when it seemed, seventeen years later, that Rhodes might desert them for a League club in the heart of enemy country.

I do not know what turned the scale to retain Rhodes's devotion to his own county and his old love. (I reject the fascinating but fearful suggestion that Lord Hawke came and went down on his knees.) However it came about, Rhodes rejoined the Yorkshire side for the 1919 season and became the main cause, with both bat and ball, of Yorkshire's winning the championship that year. His batting was as sound as ever. In bowling, Yorkshire had reason to rejoice that his left hand had not lost its cunning. Never, except in those three years at the beginning of the century, had he maintained such matchless length and flighted so uncannily. Matches were experimentally reduced to two days instead of three, and each day's cricket was longer and more tiring than it had ever been before. But Rhodes never wearied; in his forty-second year he was in his prime. In what was virtually the first county match for five years, he played as though he had never left off. Against Gloucestershire at Gloucester he hit up 72, batting at No. 5, and then took seven wickets for 47. His admirers called this an 'all-round triumph', but he had not finished yet. When Gloucestershire followed on, he was not called on to bowl till half the side were out. At the end of the innings his analysis read:

Overs	Mdns	Runs	Wkts
3·3	1	5	4

He had hurried Yorkshire along to an innings victory in twenty-one balls.

All through the season he was, so to speak, pulling something out of the hat. If it was not a hard-hit 135 against Hampshire or a truly brilliant 78 not out against Leicestershire, it was any one of a whole string of irresistible bowling feats: eight for 48, or eight for 44; and if these exploits constituted more or less the slaughter of such innocents as Northants and Warwickshire, he was not taking 'money for jam' when he came to take seven for 47 against Notts, ten for 122 in two innings against Middlesex, and five for 46 in a game in which Yorkshire were severely beaten by Sussex. It goes without saying that he came out top of the first-class averages, and was plainly the leading bowler in the country. The astonishing Rhodes was, with confident assurance, launched upon his third career.

III

Is success a dull thing? Does a tale of almost continuous triumph begin to pall? Not for a Yorkshireman. In 1920 Derbyshire were Rhodes's whipping-boys. In the second

innings of the home game at Bramall Lane his figures were
positively frightening:

Overs	Mdns	Runs	Wkts
8	6	2	4

But this was a mere preliminary attack. In the return game
he started with four for 20 in the first innings and then went
on in the second to:

Overs	Mdns	Runs	Wkts
17	7	24	7

This included a hat-trick, but Rhodes did not often in-
dulge in hat-tricks, which suggest a violent culmination of
effort in three tremendous deliveries. Rhodes's policy was
to keep up an even and relentless pressure all the time.
Beside this, his three wickets for 11 and five for 16 against
Northamptonshire seemed a small affair. There were one or
two matches of all-round excellence, such as gave him his 78
with the bat and six for 28 with the ball against Worcestershire and 63 not out plus five for 56 and six for 73 against
Hampshire. In this game he completed his eleventh double.
In spite of his consistency, there were times when his sterling
efforts did not bring victory to his side. Thus he wrought
valiantly against Surrey at Sheffield, and yet Yorkshire lost
by over 200 runs, and Fender, who scored 56 in twenty
minutes, hit him for 21 in an over. His seven wickets for 53
against Middlesex also taken in vain, for Yorkshire, after a
palpitating struggle, failed by four runs to save the game.
Rhodes, in short, was even at his greatest, fallible enough to
be human. But only just.

In the autumn of that year he set out on his fourth and last
tour of Australia. This M.C.C. side, courageously led by
J. W. H. T. Douglas, endured the roughest handling that

any tourists had ever had, and lost only five Test matches because they played only five. Douglas was indomitable and Hobbs was his shining self, but the rest of the team seldom rose above the fairly good. Misfortunes apart, and this was a most unlucky side, the main reason for their rout was not so much their inadequacy on the field as their opponents' strength. Those at home who felt that the tourists were curling up and dying far too easily had their eyes opened to the truth when the magnificent Australian team of 1921 came over and buried the remains of England's pride which they had slaughtered some months before. The fact is: Australia, as she was to do again, had recovered far more quickly from the ravages of war (which, to speak fairly, did not ravage her quite so violently).

As for Rhodes, he did little better, though no worse, than most of the others, He succeeded in reaching his 1,000 runs for the tour, but a sizable part of this total came from two big efforts: 162 against Queensland at Brisbane, where Rhodes in tropical heat batted as sedately as though the cool breezes of an English spring time had been playing round him; and 210 against South Australia in the last game of the tour. Apart from a skilful six for 39 against Victoria on the sort of Melbourne 'sticky dog' that he had exploited so ruthlessly seventeen years before, his bowling achieved little to write home about. Though he took 29 wickets in all, only four of them were in Tests and these cost over 60 runs apiece. His batting in Test matches only once rose to his own high standards. This was an honest fighting innings of 73 which bravely attempted, but failed, to save the fourth Test. The rest may be fairly regarded as failure. Furthermore, he was twice run out in Test matches, which was rather as though a fanatical teetotaller had suddenly been convicted of drunkenness. If this showed human fallibility, he was human indeed.

IV

In 1921 English cricket still lay in the trough of the wave. She had many good cricketers and a few great ones, including Hobbs, Woolley, and Rhodes himself; what seemed difficult to the point of impossibility was the task of finding and welding together a coherent eleven. The selectors, handicapped by the illness of Hobbs and by slightly lesser evils, thrashed about like so many wounded whales and, before the Test series ended, called in all on a number of players that was only a little smaller than three elevens. The Australians won the first three Tests with almost arrogant ease, and if they did not have the best of the draw in the remaining two, they gave the impression that they could easily have exerted themselves a good deal more if they had thought the effort worth while.

Rhodes might have felt, had he wished to be disdainful, that he had little part or lot in these disasters. After the first Test, in which he made 19 and 10 and took two wickets for 33, he was dropped in favour of what (Yorkshire supporters said) were in effect hordes of untried players. It was suggested that he had lost his place because he regarded the fast bowling of McDonald and Gregory, and the prospect of permanent injury therefrom, with some distaste. (Who, in heaven's name, did not?) Yet the selectors might usefully have remembered that, earlier in the month, Rhodes had taken seven Australian wickets for 89 for Yorkshire on a batsman's pitch and then gone on to score 63 courageous runs on one favourable to the bowlers. In this game he batted valiantly against an attack that contained McDonald, if not Gregory. The harassed selectors, Yorkshire folk declared, might have persevered with this all-rounder a little longer. Rhodes expressed his feelings on the situation in the best, perhaps the only, way open to a cricketer and a gentleman. On the day England began the second Test at Lord's without him, he played, for Yorkshire against Leicestershire, the highest innings of his career. You would have thought that a score of 267 not out, studded with thirty fours, was effort enough for any one game. But not for Rhodes. When Leicester went in and then followed on, he stood out as the most effective bowler in each innings, and his combined bag was seven for 66.

'That'll larn 'em!' cried the population of the Ridings in one colourful collective howl.

As it happened, even this severe lesson did not *larn* the selectors, who staggered along to their doom without picking Rhodes again. He, in his turn, went on serenely to enjoy one of the most cheerful county seasons of his lifetime. He did not quite head the first-class bowling figures, as he had done in 1919 and 1920, but in reaching and holding second place he enjoyed the satisfaction of knowing that he had only been beaten by a short head by his county colleague, E. R. Wilson, and that he had taken three times as many wickets as Wilson, anyhow.

He scored two other centuries in the season besides that monumental 267, and all three were not out. As for bowling, he was unceasingly capable on a good wicket of slowing down or tying up the most aggressive batsman and, on a drying pitch, of beguiling any side in the country to their fate. He could take four for 30 and five for 74 against Notts; and five for 27 against Sussex. The two feats which added up to his best performance were his bowling and batting against Surrey at the Oval, where he took six wickets for 38 and then went on to score a faultless 65. Seldom had even he either bowled or batted better.

It was in this year that Rhodes in his batting adopted what was afterwards called 'the two-eyed stance'. The phrase, like so many catch-phrases, is a foolish one, because a batsman should presumably use both his eyes whichever way he stands. The stance itself was inelegant but effective for its own purpose. He was in his forty-fourth year and he may well have felt that he was not quite nippy enough in his footwork to deal with the extremely fast bowling of post-war cricket. He may even have felt, consciously or half-unconsciously, the first intimation that his wonderful eyesight was growing a little less than perfect. At any rate, if people said he could not play Gregory and McDonald, he would show them how it could be done. His new stance, instead of being exactly at right-angles to the bowler, was inclined to the leg-side, with the left shoulder pointing toward mid-on. Purists who worshipped the lordly sweep and graceful flowing movement of a Palairet or an R. E. Foster felt that an outrageous blow was being struck to every aesthetic canon. How could a man bat in that cramped, ugly style? Did he think he was playing French cricket, or what? But Rhodes held his ground, maintaining (with a straight face) that he only did it so as not to risk giving catches in the slips. The new method would cut him off from many of the more beautiful off-side strokes, but he was more concerned with utility than with beauty. It was from now on that he felt free to follow his famous dictum: 'The cut isn't a business stroke.'

This is no place to discuss, excuse or abuse, the two-eyed stance. At its worst, it could become a method of using the bat as a third pad, as though the batsman were a hockey-goalkeeper deprived of his stick. At its best, as Rhodes intended, it was a reinforced method of defence in time of trouble—and English batsmen in 1921 were almost permanently in trouble. Moreover, it could be a source of truly powerful scoring shots on the on-side. But just as the naturalness of Gerald Du Maurier and the subtle and sensitive under-acting of John Geilgud brought a horde of pretentious inaudibles and mumping mumblers on to the stage in their train, so Rhodes's new businesslike methods encouraged pad-play of the most pernicious kind in lesser men. It is the eternal story of the pioneer whose disciples do his gospel more harm than his sworn enemies.

Two-eyed stance or no two-eyed stance, Rhodes went triumphantly through the season of 1922. He came out at the top of the first-class bowling averages for the third time in four. In batting, his average was only a tiny fraction under 40 and the prolific Sutcliffe was the only Yorkshireman who stood above him. In going to the wicket sometimes at No. 5 and sometimes No. 6, he scored four centuries, and without question formed the backbone of the middle batting. Occasionally critics complained that Yorkshire's batting, and especially that of Rhodes, lacked the quality of attractiveness. Frankly, Rhodes would not have cared twopence for criticism of this kind. He would have applauded, if he had ever heard it, Wellington's dictum: 'Bony always wanted me to give him a nice big battle; my inclination was to disoblige him.' His job, as he conceived it, was not to bat in a showy and spectacular manner. It was to ensure that enough runs were put on the board to make certain that the more important work performed by the bowlers should not be wasted. This may not have been the highest of ideals, but it was typical of the Yorkshire of the period, and a majority of Yorkshire spectators wholeheartedly approved of it. Moreover, it was almost uniformly successful.

Of his bowling it should be said that at its best it was magnificent. Those who declared that some of his most sensational feats, such as four for 6 against Northants and five for 12 against Warwickshire, were carried out at the expense of the poor and lowly, spoke the truth but not the whole truth. A more important consideration was that he was engaged in building up, by counsel and example, the most powerful and versatile attack ever controlled by any county. The only attack to be compared with that of the Yorkshire of the early nineteen-twenties is the present-day Surrey combination, a formidable phalanx, bristling with hostility: Lock, Laker, Loader, and the Bedsers. There is no armour that cannot be pierced by one or other of these weapons, fierce or insidious. The Yorkshire attack of the period was as aggressive and, I think, more varied. There is not a name among them that does not conjure up some terror to batsmen far beyond the reputation of ordinary bowlers: Waddington, fast left-hand, with one of the most beautifully rhythmic actions ever seen; Roy Kilner, slow left-hand, with a touch of the old magic of Peate and Peel; Macaulay, almost the most aggressive bowler who ever lived, who willed the end of each batsman as though solemnly cursing him; Emmott Robinson, with the funny little hop in the middle of his run, vying with Macaulay in passionate aggression; and, when the summer vacation began, E. R. (Rockley) Wilson, urbane, cultured, almost apologetic and, as a bowler, deceptive and deadly. And, behind them all, planning their campaigns and directing their onslaughts was the wise, tough old general, Wilfred Rhodes. Never had bowling such an imperial general staff and never had staff such a chief.

What a company of warriors they were! The tales of George Macaulay's ferocity are legion. It was to him an insult and an offence that the batsman should survive any given ball. If he had had a wax image of the batsman, he would have riddled it with red-hot knitting needles. His appeal for leg-before-wicket was the frenzied demand of a public prosecutor for the maximum penalty. (Even so did Robespierre demand the guillotine for his former friends.) It was to him that the almost equally famous umpire, Bill Reeve, observed: 'There's only one man ever made more appeals than you, George, and that was Dr Barnardo!'

As an Edwardian beauty may be best known to posterity by the portrait of her that Sargeant painted, so Emmott Robinson may live for a wider audience in Neville Cardus's immortal invocation: 'And the Lord gathered together a heap of Yorkshire clay and breathed into it and said: "Emmott

Robinson, go on and bowl at the pavilion end for Yorkshire." '

My friend, Alan Shackleton, tells a truthful, if more prosaic tale. Playing as a youngster for Yorkshire against Cambridge University, he was posted at cover-point during Emmott's slaughter of the innocent undergraduates. The score was about five for 16. Suddenly a bolder spirit, Walter Robins by name, slashed a ball to cover. It came like a bullet at Shackleton's ankles. With a wild dive he half stopped it. Spinning madly, it eluded his grasp, and as he chased it and threw in the batsman were scrambling home for a second run. Emmott Robinson, bowling irresistibly, finished off the rest of the side as though shelling peas. As the fieldsmen walked in, Billy Ringrose, now Yorkshire's scorer, called out Emmott's analysis. It was eight for 13.

Shackleton, the new boy, was sincere in his congratulations. 'Eight for thirteen,' he breathed admiringly. 'Marvellous.'

Emmott turned on him with the grim fury of a man who has been cruelly robbed.

'Ay, eight for thirteen; and if tha'd been half awake, it'd have been eight for twelve.'

This was the material from which Rhodes moulded the deadliest of Yorkshire's attacks. He was not its spearhead; he was the power behind its directing shaft. That is why, although he was normally only the fourth or fifth bowler, he was capable of taking his 100 wickets in the season, even when Waddington's pace, Macaulay's fire, and Kilner's cunning had usually had their way before he began.

For bowlers generally this was a time of intense keenness and extra 'tightness'. For batsmen it brought to birth the era of safety-first. It was the time that ushered in the new kind of Yorkshire and Lancashire match, where the aim, it seemed, was not to score runs, but to prevent the other side from scoring any; not to win, but at all costs to stop the other side from winning. ('What that sort of match wants,' said

Roy Kilner, 'is no umpires and fair cheatin' all round.') A stranger might have thought such matches dull; not so the players or the spectators at Old Trafford or Bramall Lane. Defence was of the essence; the bowler who could prevent the batsman from scoring, the batsman who could go on keeping a deadly ball out of his wicket: these were the men who deserved well of their fellows.

The return Roses match of 1922 provided a supreme example of this kind of game, which in some ways was less like a cricket match than a close-locked wrestling bout. The game was fought every inch of the way and on the last day Yorkshire were left with 132 to get to win. Wickets fell alarmingly. Rhodes, coming in at No. 5, defended his stumps with his life. The score crept up. More wickets fell, and the skipper, Geoffrey Wilson, was absent, ill. When Rockley Wilson, the tenth and therefore last man, joined Rhodes, six runs were needed to win. The bowling was obstinately accurate in length. The fieldsmen crept nearer. Even more threateningly than the fieldsmen, the darkness crept down. Five overs were bowled in the gloom and only three runs were scored. When the last over began Yorkshire still needed three to win. Rhodes played each ball carefully. The three runs eluded Yorkshire. The last ball came. Now was the time for one heroic four to win or lose it all and give Rhodes his 20 into the bargain. Down came the ball. It turned away to the off, and Rhodes left it alone as circumspectly as if it had been the first ball of the match. The temptation to sinful pleasure had been resisted and the policy of safety first had been played to its logical conclusion.

VI

Yorkshire had won the county championship in 1922. For the next three years they were to win it again. To carry off four championships in succession was a rare feat in that decade, whatever it may be today. To those watching cricket

at the time, or merely flipping through *Wisden* at a later date,
it must have seemed that, for Wilfred Rhodes, time had stood
still. It was all very well for a Peter Pan, a fairy child, never
to grow up; but here was a grown man, rich in his maturity,
who had reached the peak of skill's perfection in his honourable craft and by some miracle remained on the heights year
after year, as though he would escape for ever the wearying
of age and the condemnation of the years. Men indeed did
come and men did go—where were the men who had played
with him in 1898?—but he seemingly went on for ever.
Time (and its passing) left no mark upon him.

In the first two of these three championship years he
achieved his fourteenth and fifteenth doubles, at this point
breaking the record of fourteen set up by George Hirst.
I would prophesy that this record is unlikely to be broken,
partly because all-round qualities are no longer sufficiently
admired, but mostly because there are no longer any cricketers like Hirst and Rhodes. And this fact can be stated
without a single harsh thought for the excellent young men
of today. In the third year (1925) Rhodes took considerably
fewer wickets than usual, but his batting average rose from
26 to 40. At the age of forty-seven he was well worth his
place in a side where competition for entry was fierce.

When the pitches of 1923 helped him at all, the batsmen
must often have felt that it was hardly worth trying to play
him. His five for 8 against Essex at Leyton and his seven for
15 against Gloucestershire at Bristol owed a good deal to
the wickedness of the wicket, but in the game against Sussex
at Headingley he scored 88 and, in the two innings, took
eight wickets for 60. In this match the pitch showed him no
favour. His habit of all-round achievement was prettily
displayed in the game against a strong Middlesex side at
Bradford, when, amid snow-showers, he scored 126 and then
took five wickets for 29. His batting continued to be sound,
if less than elegant by purely artistic standards; his bowling

From a painting by Ernest Moore

THE CLASSIC ACTION

'There is pure poetry in the lovely curving flight of a slow ball
bowled by the master.'

'Hedley Verity, to whom Rhodes bequeathed his secrets of length and spin as surely as Elijah bestowed his mantle on Elisha.'

FRIEND OF THE FAMILY
Wilfred Rhodes with David Denton's daughter

WILFRED RHODES ON HIS SEVENTY-FIFTH BIRTHDAY

'There is pathos in old age and pathos in blindness; in Wilfred Rhodes there is no pathos, but a kind of grandeur.'

GEORGE HIRST AND WILFRED RHODES

'Who was the greatest all-rounder? Nobody knows, but he batted right-hand and bowled left; and he came from Kirkheaton.'

brought him 134 wickets, spoils that would have been worth while to his side, even if he had made no runs. Perhaps he did not spin the ball quite as viciously as in his greatest days, but his length remained impeccable and his accuracy reduced batsmen to despair and critics to silence.

The year 1924 saw Yorkshire's thirteenth championship. It also, being inclement beyond belief, even for an English summer, saw three Yorkshire bowlers take their places among the first half-dozen in the first-class averages. Macaulay was first, Kilner second, and Rhodes, who, match by match, had to be content with what victims these two left him, came sixth. Even with this limited quarry, he had some pretty pickings, such as five for 30 in a tight game against Notts, which Yorkshire only won by the skin of their teeth; six for 25 against Derbyshire, and eight for 54 against Northants. When he had an analysis of 4 overs, 2 maidens, 2 runs, 2 wickets, he merely shrugged his shoulders and opined that he should have been put on sooner. On such suitable wickets as the season provided he was as a rule cruelly difficult to play, but occasional rare spirits among the enemy would face him boldly and hit him for six. This splendidly reckless policy was carried out by F. T. Mann of Middlesex, who gloriously drove him for four sixes in one over, the first two of which landed on the pavilion roof. This was a continued proof that even Rhodes was not infallible, only nearly so.

In 1924, too, occurred the incredible Whitsuntide Roses match in which Yorkshire were left with 58 runs to get to win and failed by as many as 24 to get them. Neville Cardus has brilliantly described how this disaster left Leeds a stricken city and caused local tram-drivers to abandon their trams in silent despair. For myself I read the result in an evening paper at a country railway station. It was only when I had bought three papers that confirmation of the incredible gradually sank into my consciousness and in my distress I walked blindly up and down the patform, failing to observe that my train, like the light of my hopes, had gone out. There is a legend that, after the holocaust, the Yorkshire eleven sat in their dressing-room, too dazed to change, wondering by what evil influence (other than the magnificent bowling of Parkin and Richard Tyldesley) they had got themselves out. One of their number had, against all instinct, training, and the lessons of history, insensately galloped down the pitch and been stumped; another had lashed out wildly at an off-ball not merely against his better judgement but against the spin, only to see it stick in the outstretched left hand of a fieldsman who was even more astonished at the outcome than the batsman himself.

Mr A. glared balefully at his partner in sin and uttered the one accusing word: 'Stumped!'

There was a prolonged pause. Then Mr B. retorted, with supressed passion: 'Thee and thi fancy cuts! At *thy* time o' life.'

If this tale were true it would be further proof of the fallibility of the infallible.

Of the year 1925 there is little to say, except that Yorkshire were on top once more, that they reigned as royally on their throne in this bright summer as they had when the season was wet and cold; and that, for the time being at least, George Macaulay appeared to be the best bowler in the world, while Percy Holmes seemed, always excepting Hobbs, to be the best batsman. Rhodes batted in his own particular style as well as he had ever done. His average was higher than it had ever been in any season in England and, indeed, his 157 against Derbyshire at Leeds showed that Holmes and Sutcliffe were not the only batsmen of rich quality in the side. Considering the dryness of the season it is remarkable that he took so many wickets rather than that he took so few, particularly as in match after match Macaulay, Kilner, and Waddington left him so little to bowl at.

CHAPTER SEVENTEEN

The Mountain Peak

'Well, I can keep 'em there or thereabouts.'—Wilfred Rhodes

I

WHEN A cricketer has reached his forty-ninth year, he may
reasonably think of retiring. No doubt Rhodes considered
the question carefully, in his own gravely thoughtful way.
Each year, I imagine, he said to himself: 'Well, it's bound to
come, but let's see how we get on this year.' And every time
he said this, he was blessed by a season successful enough to
warrant his saying the same thing at least once more.

Whichever way you look at it, the year 1926 must be set
down as one of Rhodes's greatest two or three years. He
had already followed two successful careers, one in bowling
and one in batting. This was to form the culminating point
of his third career, rededicated to bowling. It was not so
much that for the fifth time since the war he came out on
top of the English bowling averages; or that he had completed
his sixteenth double, beating Hirst's record by two; or that
he could score 132 against Essex and take fourteen Somerset
wickets for 77. (He could also detach seven wickets for 116
from a total of 509 scored by the lusty Lancashire who that
year pushed Yorkshire down into second position in the
championship.) Rhodes's chief glory in 1926 was none of
these things; it was his re-entry into Test cricket a comparatively short time before his forty-ninth birthday.

The Australians that year brought over a side well armed
at all points: Bardsley, Woodfull, and the dazzling Macartney carried the batting and Grimmett and Mailey were
the leading bowlers. Evil weather dogged their footsteps as

they toured the counties and, apart from some sparkling champagne from Macartney, the general performance was not of the best vintage. England, too, as the weeks went by and the Tests rolled into history, failed to do herself justice. The first Test was almost completely washed out by rain; the second became an unavailing riot of runs scored by both sides; the third was the stranger-than-fiction match in which an Australian wicket fell to the first ball and Macartney, missed in the first over, scored a century before lunch; and the fourth ran true to the season's form by being spoiled equally by wet weather and high scoring. So England came to the fifth Test, which was to be played to a finish whatever happened, with grave fears about their ability to force a victory. Sir Pelham Warner has given a dramatic account of the last meeting of the selectors—Warner himself, P. A. Perrin, and Arthur Gilligan—before the fifth Test. A kind of dour determination filled their minds, for they knew that England had won only one Test out of the last nineteen. The decisions that they felt they had to make were hard: the first was to drop Carr, who during the fourth game had been laid low with tonsillitis, and the second was to make A. P. F. Chapman captain. They also determined to strengthen the batting by bringing in George Brown to keep wicket instead of Strudwick. (In the event, Brown injured a thumb and Strudwick, at the age of forty-six, played and played well.) The selectors' main problem was to find a left-handed bowler who could keep a steady length as well as Roy Kilner and at the same time spin the ball more subtly. For this immensely important purpose, the choice grew plainer, narrowing down at last to a man who was sitting at the table with them. There, too, was Jack Hobbs, for he and Rhodes had been co-opted on to the selection committee at the beginning of the season. Strictly speaking, it was not the first time the question had arisen. Earlier in the year Rhodes had been sounded on the subject and had told them with his usual gruff good manners that what they needed was a younger man. And now, as necessity loomed over the five men of destiny, something like the following dialogue released itself.

'Wilfred,' said Warner, glancing across the table, 'we think that you should play. You are still the best left-handed bowler in England, and in a match that is to be played to a finish it is likely that we shall have rain at some time or other. You can still spin 'em, you know.'

'And your length,' added Perrin, 'is as good as ever.'

'Well, I can keep 'em there or thereabouts.'

'And,' said Arthur Gilligan, 'you're making runs for Yorkshire.'

'I can get a few,' admitted Rhodes.

'And your fielding is all right,' said Hobbs.

Rhodes permitted himself a wry smile.

'The farther I run, the slower I get.'

And when the team for the fifth Test match at the Oval was announced, the name of Rhodes, to the south's surprise and the north's delight, was in the list.

II

The game, one of the half-dozen greatest in Test history, has often been described in detail and need only be outlined here. On the first day England batted on an excellent wicket and made the fair, but by no means massive, score of 280. There was a suggestion that the batsmen played a little lightheartedly and Hobbs, of all people, was bowled by a full toss. To do just this had for years been the dream, half-wistful, half-fantastic, of Arthur Mailey. When the impossible actually happened, Mailey rubbed his eyes and fumbled for the bedside light. He only came slowly to, as he watched Hobbs walk away. Matters were evened out when Australia, the same evening, lost four wickets, including those of Bardsley and Macartney, for 60, but England had not truly seized the advantage that the toss should have given them.

Next day Australia made a fair recovery and, chiefly through some bold hitting by Gregory, finished 22 runs in front. Woodfull, who had batted for a long time with great steadiness, was dismissed, so to speak, by remote control. That morning Warner had received a letter from a Sheffield enthusiast, who recalled that in the Yorkshire v. Australia game at Bramall Lane in the June of that year Rhodes had forced Woodfull to play on with a ball that broke the 'wrong way'. 'Tell Wilfred,' adjured the eager correspondent, 'to diddle him again!' Warner showed the letter to Chapman and Rhodes, and, says Warner: 'Presently Rhodes was put on to bowl. He sent down two maiden overs of superlative length and in the third over down came a ball, the identical fellow to the one that had done the trick at Bramall Lane.' It did the trick again. On that beautiful Oval wicket Rhodes bowled thirteen more maidens; off the twenty-five overs he sent down, only 35 runs were scored and he took another wicket besides Woodfull's. It was bowling reminiscent of his matchless effort at Sydney twenty-two years before.

That evening Hobbs and Sutcliffe scored 49 without being parted and I still tremble to think what might have happened if either of these two had been out before close of play. That night London suffered a sudden downfall of tropical rain and no doubt the Australian bowlers, wakened by the driving rain on their hotel windows, turned over and went to sleep again, smiling as they slept, serene in the prospect of wickets-for-jam in the morning. When Hobbs and Sutcliffe resumed, the wet wicket was steadily worsening under a drying sun. It is doubtful whether any two batsmen at any crisis of cricket history have ever played better. (Sutcliffe himself has told me that he thought his innings at Melbourne in the third Test of the 1928-9 tour was a better one; if that is so, he must have batted like an archangel.) Everything was against those two at the Oval, but for hours they defied the world. Their partnership at last reached 172 and every run had been heroically fought for. Hobbs was the first to go, bowled by a ball which painlessly removed his off-bail. He had made exactly 100 and out of all the 197 centuries of his glorious career none can have served cricket and his country better. Sutcliffe went on battling alike against dismissal and the risk of permanent injury. Turner's sunsets were drab affairs compared with the bruises that stippled his person. Woolley, Hendren, Chapman, and G. T. S. Stevens all came and went, each contributing his quota to the score, while Sutcliffe stayed there, as though he had signed a 99-year lease. At last he was out to what was almost the last ball of the day, limping home unruffled, the imperturbable warrior he has always been, a bruise in every limb but not a hair out of place. ('Ah, Mr Warner,' he said, 'I *love* a dog fight.') England finished the day with a score of 375 for six, and in the morning they increased this, with the help of some quiet batting by Rhodes and a thumping bit of fun from Tate, to 436. This meant that Australia were left with 415 to get to win.

It rained while the players were in at lunch and I feared (unchivalrously) that the enemy might escape from destruction. It was nearly 3.15 when Chapman led his men out to fight the final battle. Not the most hopeful spectator could have expected so talented a batting side to crumple, but fate, good bowling, and superlative fielding willed it so. The impeccable Woodfull was beautifully caught by Geary for a duck. Macartney came next, and as long as he remained Australian hopes remained with him, but a fierce slash imperfectly middled, sent the ball venomously spinning into the hands of Geary, who, had this been a just world, would have been awarded a peerage for that catch on the spot. Then it was that Rhodes was put on to bowl. His captain had remembered that he could pitch 'em 'there or thereabouts'.

III

The Australians had so far been falling victims to bowling of sheer pace, backed by slightly miraculous fielding. Now they were undergoing a further ordeal, pinned down by the curving flight and insidious spin which were Rhodes's chief weapons. Ponsford, not yet the piler up of fantastic scores that he was to become, cut a sharply spinning ball hard and very low into Larwood's hands. Collins, Australia's captain, came in accompanied by a prolonged round of cheering, but did not follow his usual custom of long outstaying his welcome. When he had made only 4 he failed to smother a classic ball from Rhodes, which turned enough to get an outside edge and passed into Woolley's safe and welcoming hands. Andrews, who followed, struck out with a powerful hit or two, but had never a moment's comfort while playing Rhodes. When he got to the other end he appeared to be so relieved that he made a reckless slash at Larwood and, to his astonishment, saw the ball stick in Tate's outstretched hand. Tate, though he smiled broadly, may well have been astonished, too. Bardsley, next to Woodfull, was normally the most difficult of the Australian batsmen to shift, and he showed something of his quality, but after a long, stubborn struggle he gave up the ghost. Once more it was Rhodes who found the edge of his bat and it was Woolley who was waiting for the ball. In his career Woolley took over 900 catches; this was one of the easiest. The crowd could scarcely believe their eyes, as wicket after wicket fell. The cheers grew slightly hysterical as the prospect of victory, the first since 1912, grew firmer and clearer. Spectators were laughing as well as cheering. Could this powerful Australian eleven really be going out for less than 100, on a wicket that was not exceptionally difficult, certainly not as unfriendly as when Hobbs and Sutcliffe had been batting on it? The answer was: Not quite, but very nearly.

Arthur Richardson, after scratching about as laboriously

as a chicken in search of grit, appeared to receive a ball from Rhodes that was ideal for hitting. Suddenly he came out of his trance and fairly pasted it to the on-boundary. The next ball, in the view of spectators and batsman alike, was exactly the same as its predecessor. Richardson made the same confident stroke that had just earned him four runs, and was bowled, neck and crop. He had been deceived and seduced by Rhodes as surely as ever village maiden was deceived by the wicked squire. With the score at 87 for eight, all seemed over bar shouting, but there was a good deal of shouting to come. Oldfield was a far better batsman than any No. 9 has any right to be and Grimmett at the other end defended stoutly. The crowd's temperature rose high and they cheered each ball, because they could not in all conscience barrack two batsmen who were patently playing a brave delaying action for their side. Chapman changed his bowling astutely, and at the end of Rhodes's ninth maiden over he put on Stevens, who clean bowled Oldfield, top scorer of the innings with 23. Mailey compiled a score of 6, which was good going for him, and then Geary bowled him. He did not give himself time to draw a cartoon of the incident, but instantly flung down his bat and seized the ball as a souvenir. Strudwick made a swift flanking attempt to grab it first, but was handicapped in the pick-up by his stumping-gloves.

I have never seen a crowd rush so determinedly before or since. They were swarming everywhere, making joyful if irrational noises. There they were, jammed in a solid mass, pressing against the pavilion railings and stretching right back to the lately abandoned pitch. More hats were waving in the air than the same number of people would ever own nowadays. There can be few days in anybody's life when *everything* goes right. England had won. Hobbs and Sutcliffe had batted like heroes of fiction. The English fielding had been flawless and more than flawless, because, through inspired anticipation, at least three catches were taken where, in the ordinary sense, no real catches existed. Those catches were not so much taken as created. A highly promising young fast bowler named Harold Larwood had made a successful first appearance and Rhodes, the incomparable old warrior, had pitched 'em 'there or thereabouts' to the tune of four for 44, or six for 79 in all, with Woodfull (twice), Richardson (twice), Bardsley, and Ponsford as victims.

The tumult and the shouting refused to die. At last Chapman came out, a cherubic smile on his boyish face. He was given an uproarious welcome but the crowd wanted more. Chapman turned and brought out the rival captain, Collins, who in turn received his due meed of applause. The crowd wanted to cheer everybody: Hobbs and Sutcliffe, the greatest heroes of the match; then Strudwick, the little Surrey wicketkeeper; in time they all came, Rhodes last of all, as the applause swelled to something like the bourdon of the sea. For a long moment he stood there, seemingly unseeing, as though his thousands of admirers were not there. Finally, he smiled. That smile was in itself an achievement, for he did not smile too easily. His thoughts may have moved—he was never one to let them stray—over a Test career that had begun twenty-seven years before, before Chapman, his captain, not to mention Larwood and Stevens, had been born. And that day he himself had been the chief destroyer of the enemy's defences. Four for 44. 'There or thereabouts.'

Almost exactly twenty-six years later I sat in the pleasant parlour of his house in Huddersfield and listened as he talked of old, but not unhappy, far-off things and battles long ago. In time he came to this great Oval victory of 1926.

'Ay,' he said contemplatively, as though judging the affair at the bar of history, 'that pitch was getting better all the time. They should have put me on sooner.'

CHAPTER EIGHTEEN

Honourable Exit

'*He had bowled at Grace and he had bowled at Bradman.
At twenty, at thirty, at forty, at fifty, he had shown himself
master of his world and his kingdom was never usurped.*'

—J. M. Kilburn

I

RHODES spent four more years in county cricket and each
of them was a good year by any reasonable standard. In
each of the four he averaged 560 runs and over 90 wickets.
This was the culminating period of his post as *éminence grise*,
the power behind the throne. Everybody knows that, between Lord Hawke and Brian Sellers, Yorkshire had a
number of captains who were alike in their love of the game
and their devotion to a none-too-easy duty, but uneven in
their intrinsic cricketing abilities. Now these matters should
not be exaggerated. There was not one among them who
did not have high qualities of some sort, and some, such as
Alan Barber and Frank Greenwood, were very fine cricketers
indeed. In 1919, for instance, D. C. F. Burton scored 254
with Rhodes against Hampshire for the seventh wicket; and
in 1921 he scored 215 with Emmott Robinson against
Leicestershire. Such scores are not built up by accident and
it is not within the powers of a passenger-cricketer to wander
in on county records of that kind.

The fact remains that between the retirement of Lord
Hawke and Rhodes's departure twenty years later there was
not a captain who did not benefit (and rejoice in benefiting)
from the veteran's wise counsel and unrivalled experience.
The counsel may not always have been given with the sun-
niest of smiles and the experience may sometimes have been

passed on abruptly, but the skipper was usually grateful. Rhodes knew, he knew Rhodes knew, and Rhodes knew he knew Rhodes knew. Bill Bowes, in his wise, modest, and humorous autobiography, has told us how when Rhodes went on to bowl, he would set his field not by yards, or even feet, but by inches. His knowledge of the state of the wicket was so scientifically precise that when he said, 'I'll go on now, skipper', this was no brusque demand: it was an accurate report on the strategic situation. It is an odd fact, too, that Rhodes, a realist if ever there was one, could have uncanny hunches that he would be successful if put on right away.

Let me repeat: exaggeration is great fun, but it can obscure the true facts. If he had his backchat with Major Lupton, it was all good fun, which both of them understood. And if he had a couple of up-and-downers with Alan Barber, a young man of firm character and a genuinely gifted leader, these ended in increased mutual respect which reflected credit on both. It was the captain's usual eagerness to accept Rhodes's usually unexceptionable advice which gave rise to the legend that in the later twenties Yorkshire was an absolute monarchy, somewhat harshly governed by King Wilfred. This is not so. But his influence was so little questioned that it gave rise to a covey of apocryphal stories which moved Yorkshiremen everywhere to their particular form of grim smile. As for instance: Yorkshire have scored about 400 for seven and the skipper, coming in at his usual modest position of No. 9, makes a nice shot past cover and starts to run. Suddenly a bell rings and the Yorkshire wicket-keeper, batting at the other end, raises his hand.

'Don't bother, Mr ——,' he says in polite if matter-of-fact tones, 'Wilfred's declared.'

There is also the legendary game which has become known in Yorkshire folklore as the Parrot-house Match. It seems that Yorkshire, having captured the wickets of their opponents' three most eminent batsmen for a mere song, found their attack held up, collared, and finally massacred by a couple of youngsters. These two, promoted from the second team and proud of it, survived by fantastic luck, hit fours and sixes off balls that would have bowled their betters and, in a crowded hour of glorious lives, enjoyed one hairbreadth escape after another. To say that the Yorkshire bowlers were demoralized is cold understatement. You can imagine how a bowler of the temperament of George Macaulay would feel, under the lash of such ignominious treatment. The language of the bowlers grew warmer and warmer until it passed all bounds and the umpire, also at the end of his tether, exclaimed: 'How can I hear your appeals with all this jabber going on like a blinkin' parrot-house?' At this stage of the anecdote the innocent listener (preferably a southerner) asks: 'But what on earth was the captain doing while all this was going on?'

'Ah,' says the narrator, who has been waiting for just this question, 'Wilfred sent him into the long field, so's he shouldn't hear the language.'

But Yorkshire humour, I cannot repeat too often, is a funny thing, and this tale, when solemnly recounted without so much as a wink or a nod, is awesomely convincing. But those who can build such amusing stories into a case-book of dictatorial tyranny are ignorant of Yorkshire folk and Yorkshire fun. And ignorance, as Mark Twain profoundly observed, 'ain't not knowing: *it's knowing what ain't so.*'

Rhodes was no dictator: he reigned, but did not rule, as a constitutional monarch, and as such he exercised the monarch's classic privilege: 'the right to be consulted, the right to encourage, the right to warn.' And captains seldom neglected his warnings.

II

In 1927, going in a little lower down the order than previously, Rhodes made as many as 567 runs; there were no large scores, but more than once he stood in the breach in time of trouble. He took 85 wickets and this was only the second time since the war that he had failed to reach his 100. Even with this reduced figure there were several worthwhile performances. While he was taking six for 20 against Gloucestershire, there was a period when four wickets actually fell to him for one run. He bowled effectively against such first-class sides as Surrey and Notts, and when Yorkshire's bowling was subjected to an orgy of savage punishment from Hampshire, Rhodes bore the heaviest weight upon his shoulders. In a vast 500-odd total, of which George Brown made 210 and Mead 183, Macaulay took none for 100 and Waddington none for 102, but Rhodes's effort brought three for 120. In these later seasons those who had criticized his earlier change from bowling to batting, praised his return to bowling and admired his ability which was so slow in its decline that it hardly seemed to be declining at all. In this season the county club gave him a Testimonial which amounted to £1,821. It was a long time since his official Benefit in 1911, and if ever a professional cricketer deserved a reinforced reward it was Wilfred Rhodes.

Before the opening of the 1928 season Yorkshire suffered a tragic blow. The talented and lovable Roy Kilner, returning after a winter coaching engagement in India, contracted enteric fever and died soon after landing. Apart from the loss of a splendid cricketer and a genial companion, this tragedy left a big gap in Yorkshire's line of attack and more work by sheer necessity fell on Rhodes. As a bowler he plied his destructive trade with inexhaustible skill. If he did not spin quite so viciously as of old, there was still not a man in England to touch him for length, direction, and craft, in both senses of the word. If knowledge is power then Rhodes in the field was not far off omnipotence. After all, he knew, and had probably got out, every man who had batted against Yorkshire or England over the past thirty

years. He knew the weaknesses, foibles, phobias, indiscre-
tions, and suicidal tendencies of every batsman in England.
In his head, you might say, he had a complete psychiatrist's
case-book on every batsman in the country and he went
through the whole gamut of what we might, without disrespect, call feminine guile; that is, he could lull them with
flattery, tease them with increasing temptation, and finally
drive them into an act of insensate folly by pitiless persistence.
From enticement to nagging, his left hand held every wile.

There is scarcely a spectator who has watched Yorkshire
or England at any period during Rhodes's dominance who
has not seen him 'buy' a wicket for four or six runs. I have
myself frequently seen the transaction. The technique
sounds a simple thing. The batsman would be given a hit-
table ball which, with nascent confidence, he would promptly
despatch to the boundary. It would not be an obviously
bad ball, but just something that a reasonably competent
batsman could score off. The next ball would appear to be
exactly similar. So would the stroke which the batsman,
good easy man, could not be prevented by wild horses from
making. It was the result that would be different. The ball
would either elude the swinging bat and gently remove a
bail, or snick its edge to carry to an expectant slip, or, cun-
ningly 'held back,' touch off the intended drive in a fatal
arc into the waiting hands of mid-off or extra-cover. Everything, I say, was simple; the only thing that was not simple
was the infinitesimal variation that made the fatal difference
between the first, second, and third balls. That was Rhodes's
secret and will remain so.

He took the greatest trouble in handing on his private
mental dossier on each batsman to new recruits on his own
side. As the batsman came down the steps he would say to
the fieldsman next to him in the slips: 'Here comes Plonk;
he nibbles at 'em on the off.' Or: 'This chap can't resist a
nice one on the leg.' Or: 'Pitch one well up on his leg stump

and you'll have him fumbling.' One by one, he had them taped and docketed. It was an unending campaign of psychological warfare.

A young player once told me of his first county game in the late 1920s. The first time he gained promotion from the second to the first eleven, he was picked to play against Yorkshire and sent in to bat at about one o'clock, two or three wickets having fallen quickly just before he came in. As he took guard, feeling painfully nervous, he heard Rhodes say with penetrating audibility to his fellow slip-field: 'Fancy sending in a proper rabbit at this time before lunch.' A sort of angry determination swelled within the batsman's breast, driving his nervousness away. That observation made him feel that, come hell or high water, he would defend his wicket till lunch-time or perish in the attempt. To every ball he played a stubborn straight bat, and more in sheer defiance than in skill he survived the half-hour's ordeal. As he turned toward the pavilion he received what seemed a tremendous smack between the shoulder-blades.

'Well played, lad, well played,' said the friendly aggressor. 'That was a real good do.'

After lunch, alas, my acquaintance was soon out.

'Yes,' he told me ruefully. 'It was that clap on the back that did it.'

III

Nothing pleased Rhodes better than to impart to the more intelligent of his young colleagues the secrets of his bowling strategy and tactics. He may not always have imparted his knowledge with cheerful geniality, but he spread the light (among those worthy of it) with sincerity, even with passion, and any youngster who had the benefit of his advice was a very lucky youngster indeed. There is no better description of Rhodes's intensive method than that given by Bill Bowes. Normally a professional cricketer's day ends at six-thirty and if he then wishes to amuse himself, singly or with his particular friend and companion, he is free to do so. But, if he is a dedicated young man like Bill Bowes or Hedley Verity, at supper time his day is only just beginning. Around ten o'clock Bowes and Verity would be marched off by Rhodes and Emmott Robinson, as if they were a couple of juvenile offenders being placed on probation. When they reached Bowes's bedroom, the coverlet of the bed was carefully laid out with shaving-sticks, tooth-brushes and other movable objects, arranged in the positions of a fielding side.

'Now, Hedley,' one of the mentors would demand, 'what did you do wrong today?'

Probably Hedley (or it might be Bill) was unaware that he had done anything wrong that day. He may even have flattered himself into thinking that he had done pretty well. Nevertheless, whatever the bowler may have felt and however handsome his figures might have been, the day's cricket had to be mulled over, like a recording with running commentary, from the first ball to the last; the field had to be placed and replaced, and the daily lesson had to be learnt by heart. (Does any bowler now playing practise setting a field on his quilt and does any veteran now help youngsters with such fiercely loving care?) It was a hard school but it was a magnificent education.

In the decade between Rhodes's retirement and the outbreak of the second World War, Yorkshire cricket, under the captaincy of Brian Sellers, was launched upon a remarkable renaissance, winning the championship half a dozen times and building up a reputation as high as any the county had previously enjoyed, even in its greatest days. There was fine captaincy and brilliant batting, but the central dynamic power was supplied by the bowlers, and especially by Bowes and Verity, those two apt pupils who had sat at the feet of Rhodes and Emmott Robinson. If ever a torch burned with a pure gem-like flame it was the torch handed on by Wilfred Rhodes to Hedley Verity.

IV

In 1928, as we have seen, Rhodes had lost astonishingly little
of his skills. He was now batting, and batting comfortably,
in the No. 7 position. His not-out 100 against Worcestershire
was a fine, solid contribution to a match of vast scores. His
cunning as a bowler was the cunning of the veteran hunter,
who knew every trick of fieldcraft. He was far and away,
without question, the head of his county's bowling. Some
of his feats with the ball were achieved against counties which
normally stayed on the middle rungs of the ladder: seven for
55 against Derbyshire and ten for 87 as a match analysis
against Leicestershire. But his finest feat of sustained craft
and cunning was performed at Lord's. Middlesex followed
on, and if Yorkshire were to force a win, they must dismiss
their opponents by six o'clock on the third day. At five
minutes past five the last man was caught and Rhodes
had taken his seventh wicket of the innings for 39. The
Lord's crowd, less partisan than some, cheered him gener-
ously. It was applause due to a master.

The season of 1929 saw him once more head of the
county bowling. Yorkshire shared the second place in the
championship with Lancashire. Batting at No. 8, Rhodes
had few big scores but, as he showed with his 53 not out
against Kent, he could pull out an obstinate innings at a
vital point. Against Warwickshire, Yorkshire were set a
modest total of 175 to get and made exceptionally heavy
weather of getting them, but, when six wickets were down,
Rhodes joined Sutcliffe and, though dead lame, helped him
to make victory certain. There was a game, too, with Notts,
in which Yorkshire lost four wickets for 37 and, after a temporary recovery, six for 130. Then Rhodes (No. 8) joined
Holmes, who had been batting with his own personal brand
of jaunty brilliance, and by the time they were parted 247
handsome runs had been added at good speed. Rhodes was,
even at this late day, a difficult fellow to move.

With a bag of 100 wickets, good deeds had obviously been frequent: two of them at least were in the class of exploit that had astonished the cricket world in young Rhodes's first season over thirty years before. In the earlier game against Notts he bowled with all the accumulated cunning of those thirty years to take seven wickets for 38. The other tribute was ruthlessly levied on Essex, a county which had frequently been the object of his suavely sinister intentions. Admittedly the pitch was one after his own heart, which virtually placed the batsman in the position of a cat on a hot tin roof. At one point he immobilized—almost paralysed—the opposition to such an extent that his takings registered seven for 14; then, with the score at eight for 24, Hipkin came in and, in a series of violent if unscientific blows, quickly scored 43 runs, half of them off Rhodes. Nevertheless, when he was out, caught by Oldroyd, no more runs were added and Rhodes's figures, despite Hipkin's hammering, finished at nine for 39.

In between 1929 and his last season in first-class cricket he paid a pleasant visit to the West Indies with an M.C.C. team led by F. S. G. Calthorpe. The tour, played out under brilliant skies, was something of a picnic for the batsmen—Hendren and Sandham made half a dozen centuries each and George Headley made four—and the bowlers on both sides had a thin time. Pitches were almost uniformly iron-hard and about as responsive to spin as the armour-plate of an old battleship. Only the most accurate of bowling stood a chance of survival This being so, there is a certain fitness in the fact that in all matches Rhodes should be the most successful bowler. His unappeasable persistence brought him forty-one wickets, and only Voce, who paid a higher price for his, took more.

Rhodes greatly enjoyed this, his last representative tour. Lieut.-Col. (then Captain) R. T. Stanyforth, who went out with this team to keep wicket, told me that Rhodes drew pleasure from contact with the crowds and the variety of the moving Caribbean scene. Stanyforth and Rhodes were sitting one evening in the lounge of the big hotel in Port of Spain, Trinidad. A large tourist ship had disgorged a gaggle of passengers and they crowded noisily in, bedecked in the rather bizarre manner of tourists all the world over. Stanyforth felt that these sights and sounds were all very well, but that they could not be endured beyond a certain point.

'I am going, Wilf,' he said. 'I can't bear this any longer.'

'I think I'll bide a bit,' said Rhodes. 'After all, there's nowt so interesting as folks.'

It was a genuine sentiment. As he neared the end of his cricket career, he could look serenely back on two things. There was, first and foremost, his cool determined concentration on the job in hand; the other was his continuous close observation of his fellow-players and of his fallible fellow-creatures in general. These were among the secrets of his success. 'There's more in bowling than just turning your arm over,' he once told me. 'There's such a thing as observation.' After all, no man can take over 4,000 wickets without a deep knowledge, founded on observation, of human nature and its inevitable frailties.

V

The season of 1930 was his last in first-class cricket. At the end of it he retired, honourably and under no sort of compulsion. He was nearing his fifty-third birthday, but his movements were still lithe and neat, and his eye, with only an occasional warning of the future, was still clear. His record for the season of 73 wickets and nearly 500 runs was an admirable one in its own right and not such as to hasten a player's retirement. One or two 'bits' of bowling were as meritorious as anything he had done for a long time. Against the Cambridge University eleven, whose players were considerably less than half his age, he took seven first-innings wickets for 39, and against a strong Gloucestershire side, which eventually came second in the championship, he took four for 53 and four for 21. This was the year of the great Don Bradman's first visit to England and the result was a triumph both for the Australians as a side and for Bradman himself. Rhodes expressed to me an admiration for Bradman that was both sincere and rare in the sense that high praise has always been difficult to extract from him. Normally, his sense of perfection will hardly ever permit him to describe a very good player as more than good or a good player as more than 'middling'. From this opinion three men have always been excepted: Hobbs, Trumper, and Bradman, and the greatest of these, in his judgement, is Bradman.

'I've no doubt in my own mind,' Rhodes told me, 'who was the best, and I've bowled against a few.' (He might among the few have included Fry, Ranjitsinhji, Jessop, Hill, Noble, Macartney, Hobbs, Woolley, Mead, and Hammond.) 'It was Bradman. Why, I've seen him come in and put the first ball he received straight back past the bowler for four. And the second. And the third. Twelve runs, just like that. Every ball was a good one and the strokes were not really attacking strokes. But you should have seen the sheer power of them.'

I think there was a genuine affinity between these two men, at least in their sheer strength of character and their unmatched power of concentration.

It was only fitting that Rhodes's best bowling in his last season should be against the Australians. In each of the games in which he took part against those formidable invaders he bowled with such accuracy that, while they made big or biggish totals, scoring automatically slowed down while he had the ball. At Sheffield, where Woodfull built up a solid century and Bradman hit a furious 78, Rhodes's three wickets were the least costly of the day until Leyland went on and chopped off the enemy tail. In the return game at

Bradford, where Ponsford indulged in one of his run-piling orgies, Rhodes, with three for 49, was at any rate the least unsuccessful Yorkshire bowler.

The last match of the season was played at Scarborough between H. D. G. Leveson-Gower's eleven and the departing Australians. It was a sad game, because end-of-season games, with no prospect of cricket for half a year, are always sad; there was also an exasperating interference by rain at moments when a good finish might have been ensured; and, most melancholy of all, it was Rhodes's last match.

Leveson-Gower had collected a strong side and the Australians had to struggle to get in front of their comparatively modest total. Kippax batted with that elegance which always made watching him a pleasure, and Bradman made a high-spirited effort to secure his eleventh century of the tour, failing by only four runs. The wicket, drying quickly after rain, was troublesome and the ball was greasy; the great man, setting out to knock the bowlers off their length, was missed three times, each time off the *other great man*. It was, if you have a feeling for such things, a dramatic point in cricket history, enshrining Rhodes's last game and the end of the first of Bradman's four campaigns of conquest. Rhodes, who had bowled against Grace, bowled in this last game against Bradman. Their respect for each other was deep: in iron purposefulness and superb technical ability they had at least two further qualities in common. 'At Scarborough,' said Bradman, 'I enjoyed batting against none other than Wilfred Rhodes, who played Test cricket for England long before I was born.' And, as we have seen, Rhodes reckoned Bradman the greatest of all the batsmen he had known.

'Mind you,' he said, 'if mid-off had been on his toes that day, I'd have had him first ball.'

So, despite the lure of those three chances, he did not get Bradman's wicket. Of the other wickets that fell, however, he took five. Oldfield, the Australian stumper, was injured and could not bat, and Wall at No. 10 was the last man in. Off the fifth ball of Rhodes's thirty-first over he cocked up a catch to Wyatt and the innings was ended. Rain had spoiled any chance of a finish, and though the English players, notably Hobbs and Leyland, had some fun with the bat on the third day, there was no time for the Australians to go in again. Rhodes's fifth wicket, therefore, was his last in first-class cricket. He may have looked back on his first tour abroad of twenty-seven years before, when he had taken a wicket with his first ball on Australian soil. Now the wheel had come full circle and with the last ball of his career he had also taken an Australian wicket. Between these two captures had stretched a cricketing life the like of which only one other had equalled. The cheers that greeted the capture of that wicket—this incredible Yorkshireman's four thousand one hundred and eighty-seventh—were a tribute to one who, W. G. Grace apart, was without question the most astounding phenomenon the cricket world had ever seen.

CHAPTER NINETEEN

The Complete Cricketer

'Flight was his secret, flight and the curving line, now higher, now lower, tempting, inimical; every ball like every other ball, yet somehow unlike; each over in collusion with the others, part of a plot.'—Neville Cardus

I

ALBERT KNIGHT, that sterling old Leicestershire batsman, wrote a book (in the days when cricketers wrote their own books) called *The Complete Cricketer*. It was an excellent book of instruction in batting, bowling, fielding, and all the known art and science of the game. If ever there was a *complete* cricketer, it was Wilfred Rhodes: bowler, batsman, fielder, and strategist. In *Wisden's* tables of batsmen who have scored 30,000 runs and bowlers who have captured 2,000 wickets only four names appear in both: W. G. Grace, Woolley, Hirst, and Rhodes. The first two of these are above Rhodes in the batting, but their bowling positions are much lower. As for the bowling table, Rhodes leads the field— Eclipse first and the rest nowhere. As a bowler his achievements were unique, both in quantity and quality. Nobody ever approached his total of 4,187 wickets; in fact, nobody but that remarkable bowler, 'Tich' Freeman, Charlie Parker, J. T. Hearne, and himself have reached as many as 3,000. Moreover, nobody could possibly call the other three bowlers all-rounders. I doubt if all the runs of their combined careers would add up to a fifth of Rhodes's. As for quality, it is an aesthetic experience merely to have seen Rhodes bowl. Admiration for his bowling has been of two kinds: the pleasure given by the sheer beauty of his action and the satisfaction that comes from watching one who must have been, in absolute effectiveness, the most successful bowler cricket has ever known. Cardus speaks in a poet's terms of 'the curve of a slow ball bowled by Rhodes' and there is a classical portrait of his delivery which shows his perfect blend of grace and power. Hedley Verity, that handsome, intelligent bowler to whom Rhodes bequeathed his secrets of length and spin as surely as Elijah bestowed his mantle on Elisha, has described the older man's perfection in action: the left foot behind the bowling crease, the right foot out on the off-side. Then, just before the left arm comes over to deliver the ball, the batsman catches a glimpse of the bowler's right shoulder-blade.

'The ball is spun on a line from mid-on to third man. On delivery, the wrist turns and the knuckles go up and out from the hand, the ball being spun from the first finger. The momentum of run-up, through arm, shoulder, body, and turn of wrist, goes into the action, the bowler following through automatically, up and over his front foot.'

In such an action there is both ease and power, and the curving flight, with the ball travelling upwards from his fingers, takes the spin better than any straight flight.

C. B. Fry, who knew more about cricket as a science than any man who ever lived, except perhaps Sir Donald Bradman, described the general effect of Rhodes's delivery upon his potential victim: 'How does the batsman see Wilfred Rhodes? Hostile meaning behind a boyish face, ruddy and frank; a few such easy steps and a lovely swing of the left arm, and the ball is doing odd things at the other end: it is pitching where you do not like it, you have played forward when you do not want to—you have let fly when you know you ought not; the ball has nipped away from you so quickly; it has come straight when you expected a break; there is discomfort.'

For the fallible human batsman, at whatever stage of his

innings, there was discomfort indeed. Rhodes formed the middle and (I think) the peak, of that majestic, almost royal, line of Yorkshire's slow left-handers. There was Peate, who began his career as a member of a troupe of cricketing clowns and gained a kind of clownish immortality by getting out in the notorious Ashes match of 1882 ('I couldn't trust Mr Studd'); there was Peel, Yorkshire's equivalent of Johnny Briggs, the brilliant if erratic all-rounder who was the hero of at least one Test match in Australia but who was obliged to retire prematurely in the interests of good discipline. It was lucky for Yorkshire and England that Rhodes came in as Peel went out and again lucky for Yorkshire and England that Verity came in to complete his education at the end of Rhodes's career. It has been unlucky for Yorkshire and England that, while Wardle followed Verity, no one yet has followed Wardle. Contemporary with Rhodes were Alonzo Drake and Roy Kilner, all-rounders whose high qualities may well not have reached their zenith before their all too early death. Of Verity the same may be said with greater certainty. His first-class career lasted a bare ten years, and he died gallantly in action. What he would eventually have achieved with the full power of hand, brain, and admirable character, nobody knows. The Lord's Test of 1934, when he took fifteen wickets for 104, will remain in history as his finest hour. He was an apt pupil of Rhodes in the applied arts of length, direction, and spin, and there were some who thought him second to none, not even Rhodes, among the great left-handers. Bradman reckoned him very good indeed. Rhodes, who never praised anyone easily or insincerely, thought him worthy of the great tradition and, what was even more, a pupil worthy of his own personal instruction. (Hirst, of course, was, as the county coach, the lad's first mentor, but, while the two were actually members of the Yorkshire side, Rhodes furthered Verity's education morning, noon, and night.) He did not grudge a kind word—I have heard him give many—but so completely a perfectionist was he that even ninety-nine per cent of the best was not quite good enough. Someone once asked him:

'Was there any ball that Hedley Verity bowled that you didn't bowl yourself?'

'Yes,' said Wilfred, with his usual poker face, 'there was the ball that they cut for four.'

A grim little joke, but it is a fact that when Rhodes pitched a ball on the off-side that looked capable of being cut for four, he could make it rise so suddenly that a slip-catch was more likely than a boundary. You were lucky if you were quick enough to leave it alone.

If we go back to Yorkshire's earliest days, there are records suggesting a belief that Peate, whose career was unfortunately short, was a practitioner of length and spin whom even Rhodes never outshone or outspun. Those who swore by Peate's accuracy may have exaggerated; indeed, he reproved them for doing so.

'It's all tommy-rot,' he said, 'this talking about dropping a ball on a sixpence. Let 'em try and hit a kitchen hearth-rug!'

And Rhodes twenty years later substantially agreed.

'Try the morning paper,' he said.

Peel, too, was a more than excellent bowler and had his deadly days, as at Melbourne in 1894-5; like the wholly admirable Tony Lock of the present England side, he could slip in a faster ball which the best-equipped batsmen of the time, including Arthur Shrewsbury, learned to dread. Almost all batsmen have their favourites and their phobias. Each of the great slow bowlers has had his admirers; each has had batsmen whose worst bugbear he was. Ranjitsinhji, for example, thought Colin Blythe a better bowler than Rhodes, because, he said, his length was equally accurate and his powers of deception were even greater. Bradman, on the other hand, had a profound respect for Verity.

Yet, when all is said and done and every allowance is

made for the unkind fate that shortened the careers of his competitors, there is no reasonable comparison by which Rhodes does not shine out from the rest. It is only to be expected that left-hand slow bowlers should reap their harvest in seasons of rain-ruined wickets drying under a hot sun. But Rhodes took wickets in dry summers, too, and his qualities of length and flight stood him in good stead, even when the wicket gave him no help. The richest seasons of his first period, 1898 to 1901, contained long spells blessed by clear sunshine and brightened by big scores. No one has ever been less dependent than he on conditions. He is the only bowler to have taken 100 wickets in a season twenty-three times, and even in England he could not contrive a run of twenty-three wet seasons. As for that monument of Yorkshire eccentricity, 'exceptional bits of bowling' as recorded in the county year book, Peate has seven, Peel five, and Rhodes 48. And those 48 bits plus bread-and-butter bowling over the years added up to 4,187. And with those 4,187 wickets there is no arguing.

II

It must be said, and can be repeated, that no other man ever bowled for England, batted first for England, and then bowled once more for England in the way that Rhodes did. His career as a batsman did not begin until he had made his name as a bowler, but considered by itself it was a worthy career. We know that, in all, he made just under 40,000 runs; we know, too, that in cricket history less than a dozen batsmen, and those the very greatest, had bigger totals. Compared with the twenty-one times that he scored 1,000 runs in a season, only half a dozen batsmen have scored more. Among those who have scored fewer thousands are George Gunn, Hayward, Compton, Hutton, Washbrook, and the Tyldesleys.

His batting in the earliest days was fairly carefree, and as he established his position in the Yorkshire side he steadily improved his strokes by study and practice until his style developed into that of a good orthodox batsman. As we have seen, his growing skill as a batsman caused the raising of eyebrows. When he went out to bat, Lord Hawke would remind him (and at least half-seriously): 'Now remember, Wilfred, no more than twenty.' But Wilfred merely went on his way. There is no doubt that in the early days he enjoyed his batting as a kind of illicit pleasure. As his standards rose, the noise of the grumblers died down and the time gradually came when he was acknowledged without question to be an England opening batsman. He was not as great a batsman as Hobbs for the simple reason that nobody was as great a batsman as Hobbs, but he was for several seasons Hobbs's ideal opening partner, and for at least one season, the 1911-12 adventure in Australia, was very nearly Hobbs's equal, actually scoring a greater number of runs for the tour. That was a heyday of English batting, with Hobbs to open and Woolley and young J. W. Hearne to follow, but Rhodes had no feeling other than of being among his equals. While his defence had always been strong and clean, he had no difficulty in developing the whole range of scoring strokes and he would make his runs all round the wicket without any thought of risk, or indeed of any object except sound batsmanship.

It was probably during the disastrous season of 1921 that he had the first small, unhappy doubts about his eyesight. He was then nearly forty-four years old and his movements were not quite so lithe and smooth as they had once been. It was then that he changed his stance to the one with which his later reputation was connected, but the strictures that were passed on the two-eyed stance were unjust when applied to Rhodes. He had become a batsman with a particularly strong form of defence, whose strokes were restricted in variety, but by no means in power. As H. S. Altham says in his celebrated history: 'After the war, increasing ring-craft offset the years, and the more difficult the situation, the more belligerent his personality.' His steadiness as a bats-man, not to mention his belligerency, remained with him to the day of his retirement.

As a fieldsman he was always among the very best, in the close positions or off his own bowling. In his full career he took over 700 catches and only Woolley, Hammond, W.G., and Hendren took more. He had a beautifully unhurried way of returning the ball with a smooth underhand motion, which, even from the deep, brought it like a long hop into the wicket-keeper's gloves. His skill in the field was part of his general efficiency and bore the stamp of the true crafts-man. He would no more have fielded sloppily than he would have bowled a bad length or nibbled foolishly at an off-ball. For Wilfred Rhodes there was only one standard in everything he did, and that was the highest.

III

When his contract with the Perth club finished, he became coach at Harrow and the idea suggests the most remarkable coaching combination in history: Hirst at Eton and Rhodes at Harrow. That Hirst was a tremendous success at Eton is not to be doubted; that Rhodes was less of a tremendous success than might have been expected is also true. The difference certainly did not lie in any great difference in knowledge. Both had profound knowledge of the game and any difference there may have been was in Rhodes's favour. Indeed, no man has ever possessed a richer knowledge of every twist and turn, every nook and cranny of 'the beautiful but complicated game of cricket'. The main difference, I think, was in their diverse temperaments. Hirst was so determined that his pupils should succeed that he uncon-sciously breathed something of his own rare spirit into them and, time and time again, made them play better than they knew. It was not that Rhodes was ungenerous or grudging: on the contrary, when he was in the Yorkshire side with Bowes and Verity, he gave them the coaching of a lifetime. It was his sheer perfectionism that handicapped him as a coach. He knew with clear certainty the exact right way to handle bat or ball on any possible occasion; he saw with the same clarity that the particular youngster he happened to be instructing would never do the job as correctly as perfection demanded. This took some of the pure encouragement out of the business. Yet he did not mean to be discouraging.

'I remember a boy at Harrow,' he told me. 'The sports master asked me to give him a ball or two. When I bowled straight, he stood slap in front, and pulled 'em away to leg. "If you stand like that," I said, "every time you miss 'em you'll be out." "That's right," says he, "but I can watch 'em better from here." Not a bad answer, but then he was a smart boy. In fact, though he was never much of a cricketer, he turned into a very smart M.P.'

IV

The failure of his eyesight, slow at first and then worsening swiftly, was a tragedy bravely borne. It became impossible to play cricket any longer, but he could 'watch' it with his keen ears and his unrivalled intelligence. By these means he could follow everything that went on and even when he became completely sightless, he was wonderfully in touch with the game and, to speak the truth, often critical of it. He has never approved of the fielding system which likes, as he phrased it, 'half a dozen short-legs sitting in t'batsman's lap'.

'Don't cramp him,' said Wilfred. 'You don't want to stop him making shots. You want him to make the shots—*just v'rong*.'

Critical or not, he has never grown tired of the game that

has been his life, and is still, at eighty-one, as eager as ever he was, to 'watch', to discuss, to criticize and, if need be, chastise those who sin against the light of first principles.

During the years when his sight was fading, he tended his garden regularly and he played an admirable game of golf right up to the time when his sight went altogether. My friend, Geoffrey Cockin, assistant sports editor of the *Huddersfield Examiner*, described to me what he believed to be Rhodes's last real game of golf.

'Wilfred's skill and determination were astonishing,' he said. 'I would point to the direction of the ball with my toe. "That's all right," he'd tell me, "I can just see a white blurr." Then, with no more guidance than this, he would position himself, address the ball, and drive it down the fairway, straight and true. "I've mastered that now," said Wilfred; "I can keep my head well down, because I haven't to bother watching the ball!" '

The greatest quality about him in these later years has been the courage with which he has borne the saddest of all afflictions that can befall an active man. Now, owing to a progressive worsening of intense pain, he has had one eye removed altogether. This operation was performed in July 1958 and it is characteristic of the man that in a comparatively short time he was out and about again and being escorted to matches by his son-in-law. Merely to sit beside him is a rare experience. You hear a running commentary on the current match and on the world of cricket past and present. From time to time you will receive an accurate exposition of any technical problem which the course of the game throws up. Interruptions are frequent, because there will almost always be something of a queue of old acquaintances and admirers.

'I just wanted to say how d'you do. So glad you're able to enjoy the cricket.'

'Na, Wilf, tha won't remember me, but once at Bradford.'

'Forgive me, sir, but I must be one of the last of the crowd who saw you at the Oval in nineteen-O-two.'

And so it goes on. A potentate is holding his court. His memory is remarkable. He accepts compliments with a modesty wholly free from self-consciousness. You have the firm impression that you are in the presence of a genuinely great man. Anything he says on the subject of cricket, and especially of bowling, is accepted, as it has been accepted these last thirty years or so, in the same spirit as a Fundamentalist accepts the literal interpretation of Holy Writ. Some say that while Hirst played with his heart, Rhodes played with his head. There is only a fraction of truth in this, for it would be as absurd to say that Rhodes has no heart as that Hirst had no head. There are more tales of Hirst's heart than of Rhodes's, yet the more you know him, the better you know how kindly and considerate as a person he can be. Not long ago Tom Parkin, the Bramall Lane groundsman, had occasion to walk into the Yorkshire dressing-room, and there was Rhodes standing near the fireplace. Tom had not seen Rhodes, and Rhodes had not seen anybody, for several years. 'But,' said Tom, 'the minute he heard my voice, he walked toward me with quick, sure step and grabbed my hand. "Why, Tom, how are you?" he said. 'Maybe it was a little thing,' Tom concluded, 'but I'll remember it all my days. If ever there was a gentleman, it was Wilfred.' Rhodes's humour is as dry as the dryest sherry and he will repeat with relish what he once said to a nervous young batsman who was on the point of going in for the first time to face a tough and formidable bowler:

'Ay, he's a good 'un. If he comes in from the off, it'll find the edge of your bat; if he turns it from the leg, he's got a man waiting for you; and if he whips one straight through, you'll have all your work cut out even to stop it. Ay, lad, he's a good 'un. But, think on, good as he is, *he can only send 'em one at a time.*'

There were some who alleged that sometimes in his later days he tended to play for himself rather than for his side. To this there is only one reply, and that is the one magnificently given by Emmott Robinson.

'What?' demanded Emmott with splendid scorn. 'If Wilfred played for himself, he'd still be . . . playing more for the team than all t'rest of 'em put together!'

CHAPTER TWENTY

Those Great Twin Brethren

*'There is an old saying that in Yorkshire they don't play cricket
"for fun". Well, Hirst did and Rhodes didn't. And both
were right.'—Cricket My Pleasure*

I

MANY cherished English institutions, from cakes and ale to
Gilbert and Sullivan, have come down to us in pairs, and the
individual halves of these pairs have not been closely alike,
but contrasting and complementary. So it was with Hirst
and Rhodes, who, in their day and even beyond, have
undoubtedly formed a cherished English institution. True,
they both came from Kirkheaton; they both played for
Yorkshire and England; and they both batted right-handed
and bowled left. In most other ways they were dissimilar.
Hirst was under middle height, burly and broad-chested,
gay, humorous, fiery, prodigal of his tremendous energy;
Rhodes was taller, finely proportioned, grave, controlled,
capable, through the calm precision of his action, of conserv-
ing equally powerful stores of vigour. These opposite
qualities made the two of them, whether batting, bowling or
fielding, even more formidable in combination than as
individuals, because there is no weapon in the armoury of
the complete cricketer that they did not hold between them.

As batsmen they were in their contrasting styles a splendid
asset to their side: both could score quickly or defend
obstinately at will; either or both of them could radically
change the fortunes of any game by battling their way out
of a tight corner. When they bowled together, as they often
did, their only modern equivalent was an attack by, say, Trueman and Lock. The present-day pair have my admiration,

but I still believe that Hirst had more devil and Rhodes more craft. If you were the batsman, your dilemma was cruel: if you faced with increasing perturbation the fire and fury of Hirst, you might strive to escape to the other end, where the slow bowling of Rhodes seemed less obviously dangerous. Yet then your wicket would be no safer, for you would merely have jumped from the crackling frying-pan into the slow fire, and escaped from violence to fall before remorseless pressure. You would be out just the same. Whichever metaphor you liked to use, your goose would be cooked.

On 14th July 1949 the M.C.C., with the Duke of Edinburgh in the chair, decided to offer honorary membership of the club to twenty-six retired professional cricketers as a recognition of their services to the game. Election, said His Royal Highness, was 'restricted to the really great', and it goes without saying that among them were Hirst and Rhodes.

All the recipients were modestly pleased. One said it was an honour to himself. Another said it was an honour to his county. Wilfred Rhodes said: 'I'm not quite sure what it means, but I'm delighted all the same.'

II

Nowadays, as part of the policy of entertainment by interference, better-known citizens are asked what gramophone records they would like to have with them if they were so careless as to be wrecked on a desert island. Far back in the days when people could read, a similar question was asked about books. The answer, respectable if not strictly truthful, was usually the Bible and Shakespeare. (Even present-day castaways are assumed to have these already in their pockets.) Now I like to think, unless I am flattering my memory beyond its deserts, that a reasonable amount of the Bible and Shakespeare would stick in its crevices; the book, therefore, that I should choose for my island leisure would be *Wisden's Cricketer's Almanack for 1903*. So, after a hard day's work spent in cutting down breadfruit trees to clear twenty-two yards of nice level turf, I should settle down to rest and enjoyment, confident that this volume would fulfil its purpose to reveal 'full scores and bowling analyses of the chief matches played in 1902'.

Never, since the days of little Jack Horner, has there been a pie so full of plums. I have already described the famous first Test match at Birmingham, when Hirst and Rhodes put the Australians out for 36, and the even more fantastic dismissal of the same victims by Hirst and Jackson at Headingley for 23. But even these titanic encounters were matters of smaller moment than the mighty final game at the Oval which you will know, not being ignorant of the high-lights of history, as Jessop's match. It has been described as many times as the Battle of Hastings, and almost as many legends have clung to it.

The very excitement that the game aroused was in itself strange, for England had already, perhaps a little unluckily, lost the rubber. To have been beaten in the finished third and fourth games, even though one defeat was by only three runs, after being robbed of overwhelming victory in the first, was something that outraged the inmost feelings of English cricket-followers. Some rag of prestige, some rem-nant of pride, they passionately felt, must be rescued from the disaster. As a first step toward the right road, Jessop and Hirst were restored to the eleven, and this was just, because, as I understood the matter at the age of eight, failure to bring back these two heroes would have resulted in the lynching of the selectors by angry mobs and scenes compar-able with the storming of the Bastille would have been witnessed in St John's Wood. Even so the selectors picked Hayward, who was to do so well in Australia on the next tour but did nothing in this game, and left out Ranjitsinhji, whom I would never have risked leaving out for the big occasion, whatever his current form.

Australia, winning the toss and batting on a sluggish pitch, started well, slumped in the middle and then recovered with their last three wickets, to end the day with an excellent total. Now the remarkable fact in this for cricket-lovers (or -endurers) today is not that Hirst (five for 77) bowled like a demon, or that Lilley took two spectacular catches and missed an easy one; it is that Australia scored 324 runs in a day, were subjected to all-round criticism for their dilatory play, and were just a little ashamed of themselves for their slowness. There are reasons for modern slowness, but not all of them are good. If the defence is used that modern long hops and full tosses are so much more difficult to play than the bowling of 1902, then the answer is that this slow, dull score of 324 runs in a day was made against the deadliest attack in the world at the time: Lockwood, Rhodes, Braund, Jackson, and Hirst at his greatest. It might also be recalled that C. B. Fry said: 'I never saw a bad ball in a big match.' And Johnny Tyldesley: 'They never gave us a long hop; we had to make our own.'

It rained in the night—in 1902 it *always* rained in the night—and England had to bat on a pitch so sticky that 324, fast or slow, was far too high a total for them to overhaul. At lunch-time the score was 83 for six and the follow-on seemed as unavoidable as death, but Hirst fought back with all his native tenacity. His innings was sheer essence of Yorkshire, quintessence of George Herbert Hirst. The master batsmen had all gone, but first with Braund and then with Lockwood, he dragged England back into safety just as the anchor-man in a tug-of-war team holds on and, by some force almost beyond his physical powers, hauls victory out of defeat. The follow-on was saved, if only by nine runs.

It was the bowling of Lockwood that robbed the Australians of their winning advantage. By six-thirty they had made only 114 for eight wickets and the morning and the evening were the second day. Again the scribes were scornful.

To take over two hours and a half to scratch a mere 114 runs was regarded as pitiful. What was cricket coming to? The two remaining wickets fell quickly in the morning and the England batsmen at least knew that they would have nearly all day in which to get the 263 runs they needed to win. At first the task seemed hopeless. The fate that had dogged them right through the series and especially through this fifth game stepped up its malignity. On that awful pitch three wickets went down for 10 and five of England's greatest batsmen—MacLaren, Palairet, Tyldesley, Hayward, and Braund—were out for 48. It was then that Gilbert Laird Jessop came to the wicket to join F. S. Jackson and this, as the jolly Mr Hemingway would have called it, was the moment of truth. The truth was that England, despite the pitch, despite the probabilities, despite all the known facts so far, were going to win. At first the two batsmen were steady rather than aggressive, and they hung on till lunch-time as though their lives depended on it, as, indeed, England's cricketing life did. (A young man who was later to become one of the most delightful of English novelists had to return to his office desk at this point and it was one of the regrets in an amiable life and a brilliantly successful career that he only saw Jessop make 29.)

After lunch Jackson, who had so far been the dominant partner, went into his shell to no purpose and was out for 49. Fate, shaken off for a while, was catching up again. But, directly Hirst came in, Jessop began to hit. He was a man inspired by what the poet calls 'a noble rage'. Only a noble rage could have struck such furious blows. No such hurricane had ever swept a cricket ground before, and if a speed of 104 runs in an hour and a quarter does not seem an adequate reason for half a century's fuss, remember that, under the first stress of sheer peril, he took nearly half the time to score his first twenty-odd runs. After that came magnificent release. Not even Trumper had ever erupted with such fiery brilliance.

When Jessop went at 187, Hirst took over his side's
destiny and, though 76 runs were still wanted, he rode the
whirlwind, directed the storm, and nursed the weaker
brethren. He was fighting a defensive rearguard action and
yet, accurate though the bowling remained throughout, he
never missed a chance of scoring a run or of getting to the
operating end so that he might deal with the deficit in his
own bold way. Both Lockwood, who stayed while 27 were
added, and Lilley (16) gave him stout-hearted help, but when
Rhodes came to the wicket at No. 11 England still needed 15.

So we come to the last wicket stand that is as encrusted
with legends as a bottle of old port wine with cobwebs. The
legend is of course that Hirst met Rhodes on his way to the
wicket and said: 'Sitha, Wilfred, we'll get 'em in singles.'
Rhodes has been heard to deny that these near-immortal
words were ever spoken and Hirst himself told me: 'You
never remember what you say at times like that.' There is
even a lesser legend that Rhodes was not best pleased, as an
imperturbable Yorkshireman, to be told, even by Hirst, to
'take it steady', when he had every intention on his own
account of taking it steady. He may even have felt the same
momentary irritation that the brave and loyal Collingwood
felt at Trafalgar when he is said to have muttered: 'I wish
Nelson would stop signalling. He knows *we* know what we
are about.' Wilfred Rhodes knew what he was about and
George Hirst knew that he knew.

For myself I have no doubt that what Hirst said was:
'We'll get 'em in ones.' At all events that is the policy
which, with high skill and intense concentration, the two of
them proceeded to carry out, and wild excitement mounted
and roared round the arena like a cyclone. Not another four
did he attempt. When only two of the fifteen runs remained
to get, Rhodes had made 5 and Hirst 8. Their placing was
artful to the last degree. Once Rhodes put a ball behind
the wicket within reach of Armstrong's finger-tips. The

crowd groaned in unison and then gasped with relief. When Hirst placed the next single that brought the scores level, pandemonium broke loose. An elderly clergyman, thinking the game won, leaped over the boundary, yelling and flinging his straw hat into the air. Two Australians fielded him and put him back among the crowd. Trumble lumbered up with the fifth ball of his sixty-fifth over of the match. He was bowling, as the sinister Spofforth had bowled twenty years before, with the dark bulk of the pavilion behind him. If ever a breathless hush had momentary life, it was now. Rhodes, with the utmost coolness, drove it between Trumble and Duff at mid-on and began to run. He did not stop as he reached the crease but ran on toward the pavilion, for his very life. Hirst, who had to get to the other end to complete the last immortal single, ran toward the already encroaching crowd. Hirst, the hero of the match after Jessop, made his ground and was engulfed in the surging multitude of his maddened admirers. And that, whether Hirst said so or not, is how Hirst and Rhodes got 'em in ones.

When, when shall their glory fade?

III

As a Scotsman, I take leave to admire the English character. As a foreigner, I can observe it from the right distance. It breeds men who have either humour or good temper or both, who are chary of entrance to a quarrel, but fight like devils if quarrel they must; who can show moderation in all things, even in moderation; who can abide by certain principles without nattering about principles all day long, and can do good, if not by stealth, at least without fuss.

All through this rough sub-island's story there have been two distinct sides to the English character and every Englishman possesses the two elements in varying proportions. If you lean to one side you may be called a cavalier; if you lean toward the other, you are a roundhead. Never is a man compounded wholly of one kind; seldom is he exactly of both. Generally the proportions are uneven, but the contrast of loosely assorted opposites is clear: the cavalier and the roundhead; the artist and the craftsman; the dashing and the steadfast; the gifted amateur and the trained professional; the idealist and the realist; the man with fire in his belly and the man with ice in his brain. The cavalier fights for fun and his colours are gay; the roundhead fights for duty and a country neglects the roundhead virtues at its peril. These antitheses hold good in many walks of life and often enough the opposites overlap. The cavalier is not without the roundhead's courage, though he wears its plume lightly. The roundhead is not always without the cavalier's humour, though in his hands it may become very dry. Separately, the qualities can carry their own defects. If they are welded together in a nation, the gates of hell shall not prevail against them.

Cricket has its parallels of its own modest kind. Cricketers can be cavaliers or roundheads, or a mixture of both. In a later age we have seen the plumed grace of a Denis Compton and the mail-clad defensive strength of a Leonard Hutton. With those two on the same side England's batting was strong. We can see the same opposites today in such batsmen as Graveney and Bailey, though at a less lofty level. (May, I should say, is a cavalier batsman and a roundhead captain.) In Hirst and Rhodes, cricket found the almost perfect example of the two kinds of player: individually, of the highest quality; in combination, almost invincible.

In George Hirst's cricket we have, almost perfectly displayed, the outlook of the true cavalier: gay and always attacking. An over from Hirst was like a cavalry charge by Prince Rupert. The fact that he was an honest, homely professional made no difference to this attitude: he batted and bowled with all his might and nothing he ever did on a cricket-field was without purpose; yet he could say: 'Cricket's a game, not a competition.' He thought it a game, and the grandest game. 'There's nowt like a game of cricket,' he said. But he never called it *only* a game in the couldn't-careless sense that it didn't matter who won or whether anybody kept the rules. He played the game to the fullest extent of his rich capacity; this was the way in which the maximum of happiness was to be gained; it was part of this jovial game of cricket that he should do his best for his side. That he should never appeal in a doubtful instance was part of his honourable nature; it was never because he did not care or because it did not matter.

Above and beyond his skill, his keen eye, and his boundless enthusiasm, there was that additional something in his play and person that came from nature, something that was never taught or learnt at the nets, an endearing, untamed element that was distantly akin to the old England of Robin Goodfellow and Puck of Pook's Hill. 'Something deeplying, fundamental and primitive,' Albert Knight called it with his preacher's eloquence. This it was that made Yorkshiremen feel: 'Here is our George Herbert: never mind the laws of time and space; you can't curb or hold him. There's nothing he mightn't do.' That was the touch of solid earthy magic which Hirst, along with his honesty and kindliness, brought to English cricket. And that was one half—the cavalier half—of a golden partnership.

Wilfred Rhodes is, and always has been, a subtler, more complex character. It is impossible not to admire his intense achievements which are beyond the range of any mortal cricketer, except the Great Cricketer himself. It is possible to admire even more his diamond-hard intellectual quality. A fast run-of-the-mill bowler may sling 'em down and hit the stumps now and then in a happy-go-lucky sort of way; but, if you are a slow left-hander, you are using your brain all the time. If you are the greatest of all slow left-handers, you are weaving subtle patterns of length and spin, and especially of flight, with every over you bowl. You come to know human limitations as few have known them before. As a practising psychologist of over thirty years experience, Rhodes's knowledge was unique in its penetration. Herbert Sutcliffe once told me: 'Rhodes had a kind of "touch" so sensitive that he could "feel" what the wicket was going to do or how a batsman's play was going to adapt itself before those things actually began to happen.' This was not a 'magic' touch. It was what many people respect much more: a highly developed intelligence.

Beyond his abilities and his unsleeping sagacity, I would admire even more the cold, clear courage with which he has endured the loss of his sight. There is pathos in old age; there is pathos in blindness. But there is nothing to be pitied in this blind man of over eighty, who can 'see' cricket without sight, know with certainty what is going on around him, and comment and criticize work and play with his own brand of *triple sec* dry humour. (To a recent chairman of selectors who had picked an England team which, Rhodes thought, was fortunate to win, he said: 'You're just lucky. If you picked an Eskimo, he'd come off on the day!') In Wilfred Rhodes there is no pathos, but a kind of grandeur.

The qualities of such an illustrious pair were greater even than the sum of their individual talents. All Rhodes's cricketing qualities fitted into Hirst's as fingers fit into a glove. Each was the complement of the other. There was much in Hirst's cricket that was unorthodox, individual, 'natural'. Rhodes's was a triumph of self-education, the achievement of 'genius plus hard work'. Hirst, though he would play as hard as any man and harder still at need, could relax sometimes; Rhodes, in his playing days, was self-driven by a kind of relentlessness. He would never, as Victor Trumper begged, 'have a bit of mercy'. 'When George got you out, you were out,' said Roy Kilner, 'but when Wilfred got you out, you were out twice, because he knew by then how to get you out in the second innings, too.'

Hirst said: 'Cricket's a game, not a competition.' Rhodes said: 'In Yorkshire we don't play cricket for fun.' These statements of principle are as opposite as can be, yet both have their own force and both can be right. Indeed, I cannot think of any sounder basis for the game than that there should always be men who would take cricket seriously and that there should be men who would not take it *too* seriously.

A critic whom I deeply respect has rebuked me in the past for a tendency to idealize my cricketers, and especially the old ones. This, he argues, deprives them of flesh and blood and invests them with an air of superficiality. It may be so, but I have tried hard not to fall into the error again, and I am conscious that never was flesh so real or blood so red as in Hirst and Rhodes. I have set down their interlocked stories, muttering as I wrote: 'Warts and all, warts and all.' I have striven my best to discover whether these two men—Hirst and Rhodes, Rhodes and Hirst—were as good as I thought them, and the answer is that they are. In one of my heroes, search as I might, I could find no warts whatever; indeed, had I sought by the light of Diogenes' lantern, I should still have found an honest man. In the other there have been warts, but his unchallengeable greatness as a cricketer, and his integrity as a person reduces them, and there are not many, to the size of pinheads.

Such was Hirst; and such is Rhodes—heroes of an authentic golden age. Changes have come and will continue to come, some for the better and some, as I think, for the worse. Specialization grows and specialization narrows the field. Cricket would be happier and healthier if the day of the great all-rounder could return. But there will never be another Hirst and Rhodes. (Who follows in their train?) In the end the old question and the old answer remain. Who, W.G. apart, was the greatest all-rounder?

He batted right-hand and bowled left; and he came from Kirkheaton.

A Few Figures for Those who like Them

G. H. HIRST

	Batting					Bowling				
	Inn.	Runs	H.S.	not out	Average	Overs	Mdns	Runs	Wkts	Average
1891	2	15	10	0	7·50	34	11	83	2	41·50
1892	16	177	43*	4	14·75	304.1	125	527	27	19·51
1893	35	366	43	10	15·04	826.1	348	1,425	99	14·38
1894	41	564	115*	7	16·58	833	335	1,567	98	15·90
1895	47	710	64	10	19·18	1,262.1	429	2,560	150	17·06
1896	44	1,122	107	4	28·05	1,003.4	344	2,248	104	21·61
1897	50	1,535	134	7	35·69	1,111.1	396	2,346	101	23·22
1897–8	17	342	85	1	21·37	232.2	62	682	9	75·77
1898	39	567	130*	7	17·71	347.4	107	922	36	25·61
1899	53	1,630	186	7	35·43	905.3	301	2,031	82	24·76
1900	56	1,960	155	8	40·83	583	137	1,668	62	26·90
1901	50	1,950	214	4	42·39	1,135.3	261	2,999	183	16·38
1902	49	1,413	134	5	32·11	744.5	195	1,688	83	20·33
1903	44	1,844	153	5	47·28	817.5	230	1,913	128	14·94
1903–4	17	518	92	1	32·37	324.5	73	812	30	27·06
1904	50	2,501	157	4	54·37	1,016.2	219	2,785	132	21·09
1905	52	2,268	341	10	54·00	795.3	167	2,194	110	19·94
1906	58	2,385	169	6	45·86	1,306.1	271	3,434	208	16·50
1907	54	1,334	91*	7	28·38	1,167.4	269	2,859	188	15·20
1908	50	1,598	128*	9	38·97	1,121.5	290	2,445	174	14·05
1909	52	1,256	140	6	27·30	932	196	2,306	115	20·05
1910	60	1,840	158	4	32·85	1021	252	2,426	164	14·79
1911	58	1,789	218	4	33·64	1096	231	2,796	137	20·40
1912	44	1,133	109	0	25·75	914.2	267	2,050	118	17·37
1913	52	1,540	166*	9	35·81	830.3	228	2,034	101	20·13
1914	46	1,670	146	6	41·75	500.4	123	1,282	43	29·81
1919	41	1,441	180*	4	38·94	184	38	527	18	30·33
1920	22	478	81	2	23·90	149.3	39	371	17	21·82
1921	12	250	64	0	20·83	44.2	11	80	4	20·00
Totals, etc.	1,211	36,196	341	151	34·14	21,546.1	5,955	51,079	2,723	18·75

* Not out

W. RHODES

	Batting					Bowling				
	Inn.	Runs	H.S.	not out	Average	Overs	Mdns	Runs	Wkts	Average
1898	41	557	78	9	17·40	1,240	482	2,249	154	14·60
1899	49	432	81*	12	11·67	1,518.4	543	3,062	179	17·10
1900	42	655	79	11	21·12	1,553	455	3,606	261	13·80
1901	45	854	105	13	26·68	1,565	505	3,797	251	15·12
1902	46	490	92*	14	15·31	1,306.3	405	2,801	213	13·15
1903	51	1,137	98*	9	27·07	1,378	425	2,813	193	14·57
1903–4	15	188	49*	6	20·88	357.3	92	946	62	14·61
1904	47	1,537	196	4	35·74	1,197.2	351	2,829	131	21·59
1905	52	1,581	201	8	35·93	1,241.3	310	3,085	182	16·95
1906	62	1,721	119	3	29·16	979.2	117	3,018	128	23·57
1907	47	1,055	112	1	22·93	1,067	231	2,757	177	15·57
1907–8	28	930	119	8	46·50	429.5	106	1,076	32	33·62
1908	57	1,673	146	4	31·56	804.3	233	1,855	115	16·13
1909	59	2,094	199	7	40·26	873.1	205	2,241	141	15·89
1909–10	22	579	77	2	28·95	204.5	49	526	21	25·04
1910	59	1,465	111	4	26·63	613	138	1,671	88	18·98
1911	64	2,261	128	5	38·32	914.1	168	2,817	117	24·07
1911–12	26	1,164	179	4	52·90	62	—	234	0	—
1912	58	1,597	176	5	30·13	397.5	76	1,165	53	21·98
1913	64	1,963	152	4	32·71	723	203	1,882	86	21·88
1913–14	24	731	152	3	34·80	241.3	52	662	31	21·35
1914	49	1,377	113	2	29·29	840.4	214	2,157	118	18·27
1919	46	1,237	135	10	34·36	1,048.3	305	2,365	164	14·42
1920	45	1,123	167*	5	28·07	1,028.4	291	2,123	161	13·18
1920–1	19	713	210	0	37·52	181.1	41	479	18	26·61
1921	47	1,474	267*	10	39·83	963	316	1,872	141	13·27
1921 (India)	2	339	183	0	169·50	72	36	103	19	5·42
1922	46	1,511	110	8	39·76	814.1	312	1,451	119	12·19
1923	48	1,321	126	8	33·02	929	345	1,547	134	11·54
1924	50	1,126	100	7	26·	746.3	240	1,576	109	14·46
1925	43	1,391	157	9	40·91	536.4	241	1,134	57	19·89
1926	36	1,132	132	3	34·30	892.4	315	1,709	115	14·86
1927	37	567	73	7	18·90	907.4	298	1,731	85	20·36
1928	28	579	100*	6	26·31	1,163.2	403	2,258	115	19·63
1929	32	617	79	9	26·82	1,017.3	390	1,870	100	18·70
1929–30	12	129	36	7	25·80	501.1	151	947	39	24·28
1930	29	478	80*	8	22·76	776.5	284	1,395	73	19·10
Totals, etc.	1,527	39,788	267*	235	30·80	3,186.3	9,328	69,911	4,184	16·70

* Not out

Exceptional Bits of Bowling for Yorkshire

G. H. HIRST

Year	Wkts Runs	Against	Year	Wkts Runs	Against
1892	6 for 16	Sussex	1902	5 for 9	Australians
	5 for 12	Derbyshire	1903	4 for 10	Gloucestershire
1893	4 for 11	Notts	1906	7 for 18	Leicestershire
1894	5 for 9	Somerset		5 for 15	Worcestershire
1895	7 for 16	Essex	1907	7 for 22	Derbyshire
	4 for 7	Surrey		8 for 25	Leicestershire
1901	7 for 12	Essex	1908	6 for 12	Northants
	5 for 11	Sussex		6 for 7	Northants
	7 for 21	Leicestershire	1910	9 for 23	Lancashire

W. RHODES

Year	Wkts Runs	Against	Year	Wkts Runs	Against
1899	5 for 11	Somerset	1920	5 for 18	Northants
	6 for 16	Gloucestershire		7 for 24	Derbyshire
	9 for 28	Essex		8 for 39	Sussex
	6 for 28	Essex	1921	2 for 5	Middlesex
1900	7 for 20	Worcestershire		3 for 14	Gloucestershire
	8 for 23	Hampshire		2 for 7	Northants
1901	6 for 4	Notts		5 for 27	Sussex
	7 for 20	Gloucestershire	1922	4 for 6	Northants
1902	8 for 26	Kent		4 for 12	Cambridge Univ.
	6 for 15	M.C.C.		5 for 12	Warwickshire
1903	5 for 4	Worcestershire		6 for 13	Sussex
1904	4 for 12	Hampshire	1923	5 for 8	Essex
	4 for 12	Essex		7 for 15	Gloucestershire
1905	6 for 9	Essex	1924	6 for 22	Cambridge Univ.
	6 for 16	Cambridge Univ.		4 for 16	Essex
1908	6 for 17	Leicestershire		3 for 10	Sussex
1910	5 for 5	Derbyshire	1926	4 for 15	Hampshire
1911	7 for 16	Derbyshire		8 for 48	Somerset
1914	7 for 19	Derbyshire	1927	6 for 20	Gloucestershire
1919	4 for 12	Derbyshire	1928	7 for 39	Middlesex
1919	4 for 5	Gloucestershire		4 for 10	Essex
	5 for 18	Warwickshire	1929	9 for 39	Essex
1920	4 for 2	Derbyshire		7 for 38	Notts
	5 for 16	Northants	1930	7 for 35	Cambridge Univ.

Short Book List

Altham, H. S., and Swanton, E. W., *A History of Cricket*, 4th edn. (Allen & Unwin, 1948)

Bowes, W. E., *Express Deliveries* (Stanley Paul, 1949)

Bradman, Sir Donald, *The Art of Cricket* (Hodder & Stoughton, 1958)

Cardus, Neville, *Autobiography* (Collins, 1947)
—— *Cricket All the Year* (Collins, 1952)
—— *Good Days* (Rupert Hart-Davis, 1948)
—— *Second Innings* (Collins, 1950)

Country Vicar, *Cricket Memories* (Methuen, 1930)

Fry, C. B., *Life Worth Living* (Eyre & Spottiswoode, 1939)

Hawke, Lord, *Recollections and Reminiscences* (Matthews & Norgate, 1924)

Holmes, Rev. R. S., *History of Yorkshire County Cricket Club, 1833-1903* (Constable, 1904)

Kilburn, J. M., *History of Yorkshire Cricket Club 1924-49* (Yorkshire C.C., 1950)
—— *The Scarborough Cricket Festival* (Scarborough C.C., 1949)

Knight, A. E., *The Complete Cricketer* (Methuen, 1906)

Mallalieu, J. P. W., *Sporting Days* (Sportsman's Book Club, 1955)
—— *Very Ordinary Sportsman* (Routledge, 1957)

Martineau, G. D., *They Made Cricket* (Museum Press, 1956)

Pullin, A. W. (Old Ebor), *History of Yorkshire County Cricket, 1903-23* (Chorley & Pickersgill, 1924)

Roberts, E. L., *Yorkshire's Twenty-Two Championships* (Arnold, 1949)

Sutcliffe, Herbert, *For England and Yorkshire* (Arnold, 1935)

Thomson, A. A., *Cricket My Pleasure* (Museum Press, 1953)
—— *Pavilioned in Splendour* (Museum Press, 1957)

Verity, Hedley, *Bowling 'Em Out* (Hutchinson, 1935)

Warner, Sir Pelham F., *Cricket Between Two Wars* (Chatto & Windus, 1942)

—— *England v. Australia 1911-12* (Sportsman's Book Club, 1958)

—— *How We Recovered the Ashes, 1903-4* (Newnes, 1904)

—— *Long Innings* (Harrap, 1951)

Wisden's Cricketer's Almanacks (1892-1931)

Yorkshire C.C.C. Yearbooks (to 1931)

This is a book about Hirst and Rhodes, whose names, separately or together, appear *passim*. I am, however, prejudiced against cluttering every page with such items, however genuine, as: HIRST, G. H., *bags brace against Northants*, p. 64, and RHODES, W., *asks for whom the bell tolls*, p. 101. The names of the other cricketers mentioned are set out below, but for Hirst and Rhodes it would be easier to read the book than to battle with an index three times its length.—A. A. T.

Index

INDEX

Parkin, C. H., 160
Peate, E., 104, 155, 184-6
Peel, R., 28-9, 92-4, 104, 155
Perrin, P. A., 162-3
Ponsford, W. H., 166, 168, 180
Pullin, A. W. (Old Ebor), 21

Radcliffe, E. J., 65
Raikes, T., 84
Ranjitsinhji, K. S., 14, 35, 40, 42, 46, 48, 86, 98, 105, 108, 111, 117, 127, 179, 185, 195
Relf, A. E., 69, 116
Reeve, W., 155
Richardson, A. J., 166, 168
Richardson, P. E., 13
Ringrose, W., 124
Robins, R. W. V., 156
Robinson, Emmott, 155, 156, 169, 175, 192
Rothery, J. W., 129
Rushby, W., 62

Sandham, A., 177
Sedgwick, H., 56
Sellers, A. B., 22, 169, 175
Shackleton, A., 156
Shrewsbury, A., 185
Simms, H. L., 169
Small, John, 101
Smith, Ernest, 18, 55
Smith, S. G., 64
Smith, W. C. (Razor), 62, 64, 135
Sobers, G., 15
Spofforth, F. R., 40, 199
Spooner, R. H., 55, 86, 146
Stanyforth, Lieut.-Col. R. T., 177
Statham, J. B., 15
Stevens, G. T. S., 165, 167-8
Stewart, M. J., 88
Stoddart, A. E., 18, 33
Strudwick, H., 162, 167-8
Sutcliffe, H., 18, 77, 82, 138, 154, 164-5, 167-8, 176, 202

Tarrant, F. A., 69
Tate, F. W., 43

Tate, M. W., 13, 167
Taylor, T. L., 18, 20, 42
Townsend, C. L., 50
Trott, A. E., 87, 103
Trueman, F. S., 12, 88, 193
Trumble, H., 43, 119, 199
Trumper, V. T., 40-2, 44, 49, 75, 106, 111, 115-18, 140, 179, 197, 202
Tunnicliffe, J., 18-20, 45, 46, 54, 59, 69, 113
Tyldesley, J. T., 14-15, 20, 22, 40, 49, 65-6, 146, 186, 196-7
Tyldesley, R., 160
Tyson, F., 12

Ulyett, G., 18, 30

Verity, H., 75, 81, 82, 103, 118, 175, 183-5, 189
Voce, W., 177

Waddington, A., 155-6, 160
Wainwright, E., 18, 20, 28-9, 33
Wardle, J. H., 184
Warner, Sir P. F., 48, 88, 115, 119, 133, 137, 162-5
Warr, J. J., 34
Washbrook, C., 139, 186
Washington, J., 42, 45
Wells, W., 64
White, J. C., 12
Whitehead, L., 18
Wilson, B. B., 18, 71, 129
Wilson, D., 99
Wilson, E. R., 152, 155, 157
Wilson, T. C. P., 74
Wilson, V., 88
Wood, C. B. J., 59
Woodfull, W. M., 161, 164-5, 168, 179
Woods, S. M. J., 37-8, 68, 110
Woolley, F. E., 69, 74, 80, 139, 141, 145, 147, 151, 165-6, 179, 182, 187-8
Worrell, F. M., 15

THE PAVILION LIBRARY

All books from the Pavilion Cricket Library are available through your local bookshop or can be ordered direct from Pavilion Books Ltd.

	hardback	paperback
Through the Caribbean Alan Ross	£10.95	£5.95
Hirst and Rhodes A. A. Thomson	£10.95	£5.95
Two Summers at the Tests John Arlott	£10.95	£5.95
Batter's Castle Ian Peebles	£10.95	£5.95
The Ashes Crown the Year Jack Fingleton	£10.95	£5.95
Life Worth Living C. B. Fry	£10.95	£5.95
Cricket Crisis Jack Fingleton	£9.95	£4.95
Brightly Fades the Don Jack Fingleton	£9.95	£4.95
Cricket Country Edmund Blunden	£9.95	£4.95
Odd Men In A. A. Thomson	£9.95	£4.95
Crusoe on Cricket R. C. Robertson-Glasgow	£9.95	£4.95
Benny Green's **Cricket Archive**	£9.95	£4.95

Write to Pavilion Books Ltd.
196 Shaftesbury Avenue
London WC2H 8JL

Please enclose cheque or postal order for the cover price plus postage

UK   55p for first book
24p for each additional book to a maximum of £1.75

Overseas   £1.05 for first book
35p for each additional book to a maximum of £2.80

Pavilion Books reserve the right to show new retail prices on covers which may differ from those previously advertised in the text or elsewhere and tó increase postal rates in accordance with the Post Office.